ADVANCE REVIEWS

"Molly Davis dips deeply into the recesses of our souls with this fresh look at drinking and the state of modern women's angst. Part memoir, part ode to wine, part cautionary tale, this small but powerful and elegant book urges us to explore not so much why we pick up a glass of wine to begin with, but what's going on in our heads when we pour that second, or third. She wants us to ask ourselves the same questions she started to ask herself when she realized that drinking wine was becoming more of a coping mechanism than a delicious accompaniment to a great meal. Thankfully, Molly doesn't ask us to stop or even slow down since she talks to her readers as the grownups we are and acknowledges how truly complicated and challenging life can be. She knows we are capable of making these decisions for ourselves. But, she does encourage us to be more mindful with each sip we take. I, for one, found myself enjoying my favorite Pinot Noir even more after reading this honest and lovely book. Instead of gulping it down as I sometimes did without realizing, I now consider each sip and reward a particularly good wine with the attention it deserves. In fact, as I was reading, a glass of Cabernet Sauvignon was in my hand."

BARBARA HANNAH GRUFFERMAN
Author of *The Best of Everything After 50*, Contributor, AARP, Positive Aging Advocate

"*Blush* empowers women to look courageously at their own relationship with wine. It is a vital read for anyone looking for honesty, understanding and truth, without judgment. Molly Davis shares her own story with us, making it safe for other women to start a dialogue about this interesting phenomenon. This book should be required for every woman as well as the men who love them."

SIGNE DARPINIAN, MFT
Author of *Knock Out Dieting: Create Peace Between You, Your Body and Your Food*, www.myweighfamilytherapy.com

"There is no greater act of love than being reconciled to the truth and possibility of who we are, of why we are. *Blush* is an invitation to that reckoning as only a dearest friend can provide it: one part warm embrace, one part kick in the ass. I am reminded in reading this generous book of my own forms of avoidance, my own hiding places. And I am resolved to step out from those familiar shadows with arms and hands open wide to receive myself just as I am. Warmly recommended."

DAVID BERRY
Author of *A More Daring Life: Finding Voice At The Crossroads of Change*, Founder Rule13 Learning, Speaker, Advisor

"The honesty of the conversation and how the author brings the reader into it, takes my breath away. Deeply moving."

BARBARA BELL
Captain and Test Pilot, US Navy Ret., Doctoral Candidate Ed.D Vanderbilt University

"This book is authentic, transparent and truly amazing, and as I read through the chapters, I became acutely aware that I am not alone in this myriad of feelings."

CAROL CABLE
CEO Comfort Hospice Care

"Talking about, even thinking about, how much wine is in my life is not as sexy as drinking it. Wine brings up feelings of comfort and release as well as shame and self doubt. It's a huge part of my life, though it has always been just a fixture. *Blush* has taught me how to explore my relationship with wine, to make it richer, stronger and healthier. Through her stories of life and wine, Molly Davis softens the journey for the rest of us. This book isn't about addiction, or alcoholism, it's about mindfulness and bravery. Like any brave act, it's easier to take the first step with someone you trust. *Blush* builds a trust you can dive into all the way to the last word. Like a sip of wine, reading through Molly's curiosities and experiences helped me begin to listen to, and draft my own song."

KATHY SIMPSON
Wine drinker and Product Manager for Technology and Engineering

"Anyone who has tried a low sugar diet knows the tragedy of losing that evening glass of wine. I read *Blush* in an afternoon, while drinking wine, because Sunday calories don't count. Through personal experiences and probing curiosity, Molly Davis provides a fascinating exploration of the role wine plays in the lives of women's increasingly busy, increasing pressured lives. Instead of getting into the serious land of addiction, *Blush* invites the reader to cultivate an awareness that mindless wine consumption can quietly approach the territory of crutch and habit. *Blush* encourages women to get real about their wine. Better to enjoy it, no matter what kind of day we've had, rather than count on it to get us through the rough ones."

LELA DAVIDSON
Best-selling author of *Blacklisted From The PTA* founder of *Second Story Writer's Workshop*, and national speaker on media, marketing, and faking work life balance

"*Blush* is not just about Davis' relationship with wine. It is the depiction of how a woman, no matter how accomplished she is, struggles with her role as a mother, wife, and professional—the struggles that most women quietly experience themselves. It is a book that all women of all ages ought to read and start discussions amongst themselves on how to help each other find their own wisdom and strength."

SARAH BROKAW LCSW
Author of New York Times Best Seller *Fortytude*, and host of 0the podcast series "Shared Secrets"

"Reading *Blush* is like sitting down with the author in a warm and cozy place, and having a long heart-to-heart conversation about the many aspects of life in a real and honest way. Molly Davis' voice is wise, introspective, in-sightful, melodic and soothing, and her facility to reach deep inside herself and connect so many threads from history, literature, music and social consciousness with her own personal history, is uncanny. Whether you drink wine or not, a little or a lot, we can all relate to using something to cope when things get tough rather than face what's really troubling us. Blush captures the courage it takes to face and own it, step out behind it and into being who we truly are. And that is the most beautiful thing of all."

KATHERINE MACKINNON
Feng Shui Consultant

"*Blush* weaves a tapestry of a woman's relationship with wine, love, self-discovery, life lessons and grace. Molly Davis shares her own personal life experiences while encouraging women to examine theirs, and in the process, to find their own voice."

MOLLY RUSCOE
Director US Licensing, adidas

BLUSH

BLUSH

Women & Wine

Molly Davis

Trailhead
COACHING & CONSULTING

BLUSH
Women & Wine

Molly Davis

ISBN: 978-1-942545-74-3

Library of Congress Control Number: 2016960594

Published by Trailhead Coaching & Consulting
A Publishing Imprint of Wyatt-MacKenzie

Trailhead
COACHING & CONSULTING

For Tom
The love of my life & the geologist I sleep with.
I never knew love could be this big, or life this good.
&
Haley Lauren Clare Valerie
Our four delightful daughters.
You are each in your own way…my favorite.

CONTENTS

1

A MESSAGE IN OUR BOTTLE

Why do we love our wine so much?

⌐

"What you encounter, recognize or discover depends to
a large degree on the quality of your approach."[1]
JOHN O'DONOHUE

LIVING IN A SMALL RURAL TOWN with no cell service
and more cows than people, finding and creating good
friendships has its challenges. Not one to wait for the
party to come to me I decided to get the party started,
and invited a few other women over for the evening.
Our home is great for gathering people together, with a
huge outdoor rock fireplace under a covered porch for
summer evenings, and an equally huge one indoors for
chilly winter nights. Both spots have a killer view of our
mountain. Everyone got back to me right away, and they
were decidedly "all in". Each email response to the invitation had some version of, "Besides wine, what else can

I bring?" Over shared bottles of wine and great food we started to get to know each other. Slowly at first, and over time and more bottles of wine, our connection grew stronger and deeper. We continue to love our evening gatherings. There is always some combination of authentic conversation, raucous laughter, heartfelt tears, good food, good wine, and good music in the background… Wine, women, and song at its best.

Whether meeting up for happy hour after a long day of work, catching up with a friend, unwinding after a play date, sipping a glass while stealing time for a long, quiet soak in the tub, or commiserating over lost love, lost parents, lost jobs, lost years or lost waistlines, that shared wine feels like a sacred ritual that a lot of us can relate to. "We should get together for wine sometime soon." This phrase is so familiar that it is just part of our common vocabulary. What could be better than shared wine with good friends? Sometimes nothing!

But that isn't what this book is about.

This is a book about women and wine. It is not a book about alcoholism or never drinking wine again. It is about awareness, not intervention and it addresses the murky place, somewhere in-between, "Hi. My name is…." and "Hey… it's no big deal." It is an exploration of when and why I choose to drink wine to dull pain, avoid discomfort, cope with stress, and check out of reality. And why other women might do the same. We don't need any more data to tell us that this is a topic worth talking about. We've heard it all before. Too much wine is bad for our health. It increases our risk for breast cancer and heart disease, kills brain cells, interrupts our sleep, and causes weight gain. There are plenty of good reasons to drink less wine. But maybe not good enough. Just think about the women you know. Intelligent, accomplished, talented, successful women; friends, sisters, mothers, colleagues, neighbors, strangers across the room at a restaurant, bar or party. Or maybe you. Wine has become an acceptable accessory to our often harried and hurried lives. A stylish, swanky companion, wine is like a deferential friend, keeping the truth at arms length by telling us what we want to hear, so that we can tune out what we don't.

I've been a wine drinker for as long as I can remember, and should probably go on record right now by saying I may never stop drinking the stuff. I love it. Some of my favorite memories have been created while sharing a glass or two, ok, maybe three. Oh hell, even a whole bottle of the stuff. Preferably a rich, buttery chardonnay, or a big, lush red. Gatherings of friends and family brought together for good food, good conversation, good stories, and good wine are about as good as it gets. However... I have begun to look with an honest eye at my own motives for drinking wine. It comes down to two basic reasons, which are in stark contrast to one another. One is to celebrate. The other is to check out. I've done plenty of both. Now it is time to discern one from the other so as to live more fully present to my life, including that which I would rather avoid.

When my daughters were young, they loved to play hide-and-seek. Sometimes one of them would hide under a blanket, smack dab in the middle of the room. Drinking too much wine is a lot like that. Hidden under the warm, fuzzy blanket of a little too much wine, smack dab in the middle of our life, we try to pretend that we are safe from being found by whatever is seeking to be known, felt and understood. Our life is always waiting for us, and running away from whatever is going on in our lives today only guarantees running back into it again tomorrow.

One morning, my husband of 20 years and I were sitting down for one of our morning rituals: That first cup of French press coffee before the day actually breaks. Tom is a geologist and studies volcanoes. His nickname to nieces and nephews is Uncle Rock and he loves nothing more than a good lahar. He is the kindest and gentlest of men with a soul that is deep and a spirit that radiates a kind of gentle strength. The word bedrock comes to mind. His wisdom knocks my socks off. (When, of course, he isn't being a clueless idiot. Like the time he told me that I was pretty, "most days," or as I was agonizing over the appearance of an added layer around my previously flat abs during menopause and he enthusiastically chimed in with, "Yeah, I can't believe how fast it happened.")

On this morning however, out of seemingly nowhere, he quietly asked me, "Mol, I wonder if you know how much you are loved?" What kind of silly question is that? I started to say, "Of course I do," but couldn't because of the boulder sized lump in my throat. Something shifted inside. He had obviously hit a major fault line and a tremor started to rumble deep in my soul. Like many women, I have spent a lot of my time and energy loving and caring for others, making sure they feel loved and their needs taken care of. But me? Who has time to think about that? And, perhaps even more to the point, what if my answer would hurt even more than his question? The need to feel loved is primal. Feeling worthy of love is not. How much of our life is spent trying to earn the love we seek, never stopping to wonder if it is already ours? While I didn't yet understand why, intuitively I knew that his question connected to the wine that I drank almost every night, and I couldn't help but think about Tina Turner and ask, "What's love got to do with it?"

The truth was, I had been thinking about my own love affair with wine.

Quietly.

Secretly.

Keeping my thoughts to myself, which was the way I wanted to keep it thank you very much, despite how much my husband's question had rattled me. Until I had an experience walking down our road one chilly fall evening.

It was dusk; the sun was setting behind our mountain, a 12,281 ft. high dormant volcano, 15 miles away. One of my favorite times of the day, I grabbed a coat and made my way down the road. It was quiet, with the occasional sound of evening birdsong and cows calling from across the valley. As I made my way in the fading light, I suddenly and clearly heard a voice, coming from inside of myself, quietly, slowly, say the words "Wine, Women and ~~Song~~ Sorrow," an image instantly taking shape in my mind of a book cover, with the familiar word "song" crossed out, replaced by "sorrow". The message stopped me in my tracks. Bending over, I covered my eyes with my hands, holding perfectly still for a long time, knowing that once I stood up nothing could ever be the same again. "Fuck," I whispered. "I really have to do this thing, don't I." The voice didn't answer. It didn't have to, because it was one of those moments, when like it or not, you know, in that place where no one lives but you, that you have just heard the truth. The kind with a capital "T". There was no mistaking the message. It was a clear invitation to bring my relationship with wine out of my own dark cellar into the light, and let it breathe. I decided to accept the invitation. This book is the result.

There is something called the terroir of wine. It refers to the makeup or geology of the soil in which the grapes are grown, and how it impacts the taste of the wine made from those grapes. I wanted to understand the terroir of my wine drinking habit. Why did I fill my glass or three so often? Was it really just habit? Or something more? What makes up the ground in which my mis-use of wine grows? The chapters that follow shed a light on what I unearthed as I discovered what makes me want to check-out of life, rather than check-in with myself and sit with whatever I find there.

Early in the process of writing this, I was driving to an appointment, mulling yet again over the question, "Will other women really relate to this topic?" Women who aren't living with the disease of alcoholism, but have a relationship, specifically with wine, that has the potential to quietly creep in, and have a negative impact on her health and well-being. Tired of pondering the question, I decided to tune out for a few minutes, by tuning into a favorite program on KOPB, our public radio station, just in time to hear the following statistic: Women purchase 70% of the 800 million gallons of wine sold each year.[2] And there you have it. Ask and you shall receive.

In writing this book, I didn't set out to gather data, hold focus group meetings or send out surveys. I have however listened and noticed:

❧ The woman in the checkout line in the grocery store. In her basket: a bottle of wine. No food. No paper towels. Just wine. That's all. Standing in line next to "that woman" we share an unspoken understanding of this stop after a long day for the wine that will ease us into the evening. An evening far from over and filled with more obligations, tasks, and conversations. Wine makes all that go down just a little easier. A little softer. Sometimes we exchange a quick, "My first glass of wine is almost in sight." We part ways, kindred spirits in our evening ritual.

❧ The C-Suite executive that I stop to see on the way home. Mother of 2, wife of a pediatrician. Lovely home. Totally together. "Hurry up and get here," she says when I call to tell her I am running late. "I've already poured my first glass of wine."

❧ The participant in my class who has flown in from back east for the course. "Do you have any plans for dinner tonight? There is a great restaurant on every block." (Hello 'Portlandia') "No" she says. "Just stopping to pick up my bottle of wine to take back to my room."

❧ My best friend who doesn't even like wine, when she finds a quiet moment at home in the evening, phone turned off in case an aging parent calls, again, beloved grand-babies back home and tucked into their own little beds, husband not yet home... she lights a candle and pours a glass of wine. She likes the ritual and feeling of self-care. A party for one.

❖ Checking in at a conference where I am the keynote speaker, the organizer greets me and I notice her glass of pinot gris with at least another glass missing from the bottle. Organizing those things can be a thankless royal pain in the ass. That wine? A little self-appreciation.

❖ Countless gatherings of women that I have been to over the years... book clubs, event planning meetings, church meetings, soccer moms, birthday parties, dinner parties. Wine.

❖ Sitting in an airplane listening to two women in the row behind talk about how they can't wait to get to the hotel, change into their pjs and open the wine they have packed in their suitcase. Can I come too?

❖ A good friend who encouraged me to write this book told me of a colleague of his who shared that he often comes home in the afternoon to find that his wife is already 2/3 of the way through her bottle of wine watching Oprah on TV.

❧ Speaking of TV. Tammy Taylor, Coach Taylor's wife on *Friday Night Lights*[3]. (If you haven't watched this and even if you hate football... please oh please do.) One of my favorite characters. Smart. Sassy. Strong. A hard working, family loving, straight shooting, tell-it-like-it-is kind of gal. Kind of like a lot of us. Every glimpse of her in her TV home in the evening shows her with a glass of wine. And she looks so damn good, so together, with her wine.

❧ The pediatric nurse, cancer survivor who spends her days nurturing, holding, tending and caring for premature babies. At home in the evening, she nurses herself with several glasses of wine.

❧ The friend who calls, and I can tell the minute I hear her voice if she is already into her third glass. And vice versa.

❧ A world-class health spa where women come to rest and restore; a respite from busy lives of motherhood, wifehood, corporate-hood, daughterhood, caregiver-to-aging-parents-hood. No wine until the last night when a glass is served to toast a week of health and well-being. Except that many of us have packed bottles of wine in our luggage. Our evening ritual, to go.

❧ An accomplished corporate businesswoman, with a loving husband and beautiful home, who wears her sadness wrapped about her soul like a scarf. She calls the morning after a dinner party to apologize if she drank too much wine and embarrassed herself.

❧ The morning show on a major network, co-hosted by two women. They are funny and irreverent as they cover pop-news. It airs mid-morning and rather than the standard coffee mug, each has a glass of wine. Now, they don't actually drink it. It's a prop. It does however suggest that women and wine... well, we just go together.

❧ Another friend who leaves every dinner party early because by the time she arrives she is already into her second bottle.

❧ Lest I leave myself out, a recent review of photos over the years shows that it is the rare gathering that doesn't capture me with what seems to be my go-to accessory. A lovely glass of wine. Don't you know it goes with everything darling? Right up there with a crisp white shirt.

❧ I co-lead a workshop on the topic of Contentment. One time, during an exercise, I asked the women in the room to identify things in their lives that had become a burden, things that did not serve them well. Providing them with a few examples to fuel their thoughts, I listed things every woman would recognize. "Obligations, over-commitment, poor self-image, unhealthy habits..." And then, before I could stop myself, "that extra glass of wine at night". The room changed. Heads nodded, silent acknowledgement. A sip of the air in the room tasted like sorrow with subtle notes of disappointment followed by lingering hints of shame.

❧ And finally, a friend is gone.

Dead.

Mother of three.

Grandmother of two

Wife of one.

3 – 2 – 1- Wine bottle in hand, she jumped out of her upstairs bedroom window.

Wine.

Women.

Song?

Sorrow?

Something else?

On that evening walk, as I stood at the bend in the road my thoughts gradually distilled. What is it that sends me looking for a glass of wine? What is my song?

How do I lose it? In losing our songs are we filled with sorrow, or does sadness cause our music to go silent? Or, like the musical notes of a song, are they intertwined? Perhaps we drown our sorrows in our wine, one lovely glass at a time. And in the drowning, we lose our song.

The questions felt important and worth answering, and I believe that I am not alone in my wine drinking habit: other women might be willing to join me in search of their own answers to those same questions. If they were like me, drinking too much wine was scary to think about, much less talk about with anyone else. Early in this project when I was catching up with a friend on the phone, she wondered what I was up to. I hadn't yet shared this project with many people, as I knew that I had to look at the message in my own bottle before asking anyone else to look at theirs. She happens to live in wine country, so we have shared and talked about plenty of good wine. Talking about wine is trendy. Talking about drinking it is not. She is one of those successful, articulate and so completely together and accomplished women that I couldn't imagine her relating to this "wine thing", yet I found myself telling her about it anyway. After a long silence, she quietly responded, " You're talking about me." Another long pause. "But I would have been too embarrassed to talk about it if you hadn't said something first." Most of the time we live exactly like that, in a sort of "you show me yours and then maybe I'll show you mine" kind of way. We protect our secrets, fears and pain at all costs. When it comes to our wine, if not careful, it can become too costly, depleting our inner accounts of physical, mental, and emotional currency. Thoreau said, "The cost of a thing is the amount of what I call life which is required to be exchanged for it, immediately or in the long run." When we drink too much wine, too often, what happens to our personal exchange rate?

In seeking my own answers, I can't claim to be wise. I can however commit to being curious, willing to understand my own reasons for turning to wine, and extending an invitation to others to be curious about their own. Maybe if I can show mine, you will feel safer showing yours. Perhaps this book can create a safe place to search for our own answers. I know no one else can answer those questions for me, and I sure as hell can't answer them for anyone else. Our questions are our own to live. But there is something good that happens when we choose to live them together. There is safety in numbers. Going it together reminds us that we are not alone in our attempts to make sense of things. Awareness is the first step towards change, and it seems no accident that the idea for the book came at a bend in the road. It suggests a turning point: the chance to make a new choice about wine.

That possibility alone seems worth toasting.

Want to join me?

2

I CAN SEE CLEARLY NOW

How does wine become a mindless habit?

～

"How we spend our days is, of course,
how we spend our lives."[4]
ANNIE DILLARD

IF I REALLY WANTED TO understand my relationship with wine, my commitment to be curious would have to kick in, and discovering where it all began seemed like a very good place to start. Growing up, I was the youngest of four by a long shot. Not an accident, mind you. Who wouldn't strategically plan on having another baby after your other children were 8, 12 & 13? I mean, seriously. By the time I was ten, everyone else was away at college. You might say I was an only child <u>and</u> the baby of the family. Perfect. Self-centered AND spoiled! My parents were solid folks with full social calendars and their own brand of fierce love for us. Like others in the 'greatest generation', being a good parent meant keeping us fed, safe and clean. Figuring out who we were and understanding our inner needs as little human beings wasn't even on their radar screen. I knew they loved me, and I also knew they had no real idea of who I was. As a result, life under our roof was a strange mix of love and loneliness.

The company of my parents made up for what my evenings lacked in sibling rivalry. Every night as Mom cooked dinner, Dad mixed their evening cocktails: bourbon and soda, martinis or gin and tonics. While I don't remember them arguing all the time, when they did it usually happened during that "happy hour." I remember one evening like it happened last week rather than decades ago when I was about 15. My parents were in the kitchen and I was in the living room finishing my piano lesson. Over the sound of the piano, I could hear their raised voices. The sharpness of his words, the trembling in her voice. After the piano teacher left, I tiptoed to the edge of the kitchen door and listened. Peeking in, my dad had on his coat and was threatening to leave the house. Mom, tears streaming down her face, was not saying a word, one long clear strand dripping from her nose. Like a screen shot, it is saved on my mental hard-drive.

I walked in.

The argument stopped.

Dad took off his coat.

Mom blew her nose.

We ate dinner.

I went to bed.

Case closed.

Until the next evening.

Sitting on the stairs next to Dad during another evening ritual, shining his shoes, I asked, "If two people get divorced, can they get married again?" Setting down the brush and shoe, he moved closer and hit my nail squarely on the head when he asked if I was scared because of the argument from the night before. He did his best to reassure me that he and Mom were fine, all parents argued, they loved each other, blah, blah, blah. All of which I believed. Sort of. After he went back upstairs, I sat thinking about what he had said, listening for the clink of ice in their glasses. It was, after all, happy hour. Instead, I heard a cork being pulled from a wine bottle. Back in the kitchen, I found them each sipping a glass of wine.

While I can't say if this is exactly what happened or not, I hardly remember my parents arguing after that night. Sometime later I learned that they had made the choice to stop having cocktails, switching to wine instead. Cocktails seemed to set the stage for arguments. Wine somehow did not. Evenings seemed more peaceful to them as a result and to me too. That hour actually was happy. We would gather in the kitchen, light candles, and while dinner simmered on the stove we would talk about the day. They drank their wine from lovely glasses. When old enough, I did too. The kitchen was fragrant with good food, easy conversation and emotional connection. Wine became the ritual that symbolized home and family. Who wouldn't fall head over heels in love with that? I know I did. Over the years, that ritual faded into a habit. Time to make dinner? Time for a glass of wine.

Every habit serves a purpose. Understanding the motive behind the habit is important, and the same habit can serve more than one purpose. Take exercise for example. It's a good habit, right? It improves our health by lowering blood pressure and building up bones, decreasing fat and increasing muscle, lessening anxiety and boosting our mood. Regular exercise has helped people wean themselves off anti-depressants, sleep better, have more energy and may even stave off dementia. If the motive is to care for oneself well, it's safe to say that regular visits to the gym are a good habit. If, however, exercise is rooted in the need to control something, meet some impossible standard of perfection, or compensate for the habit of comforting oneself with food rather than understanding the deeper hunger, it's safe to say it is a habit worth exploring.

My love affair with wine began at home all those

years ago. To this day, when my husband and I sip a glass of wine at the end of a day, dinner cooking on the stove, I am reminded of the best of those earlier evenings, gathered in the kitchen of my childhood. Imperfect as it was, it was the home I knew. Although it wasn't the place where I really discovered who I was, it was the place from which I came, and I loved it in spite of the cracks in our family walls.

Those who study habit formation tell us that a habit has three parts: trigger, behavioral response, and reward. Something happens - an event, a feeling, a thought - which triggers a behavior. We do something in response to that trigger, and if rewarded with a positive feeling or outcome, a habit begins to form. The first few times we choose to do that something, it is a conscious decision. On the 100th time, it has turned into an unconscious habit.

Tracing the thread of my wine drinking habit, I can see that it is firmly planted in the notion of home and family. The idiom "home is where the heart is" strikes a chord. If my wine had a name, the label on the bottle would say "Home". Wherever I was over the years, when things went south, when life got scary or uncomfortable, when I felt out of control or out on a limb, wine felt like it turned my heart toward home. Whether the turmoil of a marriage gone bad or a depleted bank account, nights with too little sleep followed by days with too much to do, toxic relationships or unfulfilling work, when I poured a glass of wine, something inside felt loved. It took me back to my childhood home, sitting in the kitchen by candlelight. Like liquid comfort food, my first glass of wine waited to greet me at the end of the day. A day that usually meant an impossible to do list, and time spent tending to the needs and demands of everyone else. Life often overflowed with "shoulds" and felt empty of "coulds." Pouring that glass of wine was something that I could damn well do for myself. And did. Night after night. One glass often spilled over into several, and as often happens, doing became a habit, a habit became a pattern, and eventually the pattern quietly folded itself into my life unnoticed. Until that evening, standing at the bend in our road.

Mindless habits call for mindful attention, and the trailhead of discovery is always squarely beneath our feet. If you are at a bend in your road, and curious about unraveling the thread of your own wine drinking habit, discovering your triggers might be a very good place to start.

3

SONGS IN THE KEY OF LIFE

What in the hell is our song anyway?

∽

"And this is it. This is the life we get here on earth.
We get to give away what we receive."[5]

NADIA BOLZ-WEBER

AS AN AUDIO-VISUAL LEARNER, I need to hear and see
something to really wrap my head around it. You might
say I'm a words and pictures kind of girl. Tell me and
show me, and I'm yours. Whoever sent me that message
on my evening walk knew that about me. My apologies
dear Messenger if I forgot to say thank you. You had me
at, "Wine, Women and ~~Song~~ Sorrow."

A song has been defined as a set of words put to
music and meant to be sung. On the road that evening
I understood, beyond a shadow of any doubt, that the
crossed out word meant our life. All of it. You know
how sometimes you just know something. Well, this was

one of those times. I didn't have to suss out the meaning, mull it over, meditate on it, pray about it, go consult with the village elder or Google it. Here is what I knew for sure (thank you, Oprah), our song is us. It is who we are at our core; the most genuine rendition of ourselves. Born with our song inside, we are here to learn the music and share it with the world. Our song is heard through who we are and how we show up, the work we do and the people we love, the words we speak and the choices we make. Our song leads us to our most authentic life, because as we sing it, we sense that we are in tune with our own soul. Our song defines and shapes our life as we follow the notes that are in sync with who we are and what we care about. When we get out of key, our inner melody brings us back into inner harmony. When in danger of getting lost in a life that isn't ours, like a country road, our song takes us back home where we belong. When we forget the words, if we get quiet and tune in, it will echo back to us from the walls of our inner canyons. It's always ready. It's always here. It's always ours. In her book, *Big Magic*, Elizabeth Gilbert writes about creativity and our pull as human beings to create. When she speaks of the creativity that comes in as many different forms as there are humans, she says that, "The work wants to be made, and it wants to be made through you."[6] A similar message in a slightly different key might sound something like this: your song wants to be sung, and it can only be sung through you.

So, how do we know the song that is ours? It can be a scary question since it sounds like it has only one correct answer, which means if we don't get it right we'll be screwed for good. Kind of like what happens if we don't find our path, discover our calling, meet our soul mate or fulfill our purpose. Metaphors like that can make us feel doomed before we start. Thankfully, our song is more improvisation than memorization, and our charge is to learn the key that we're working with, have an understanding of the scale and theme, and then run with it and see where it takes us. Good improv appears to effortlessly take unexpected turns, twists and riffs. But don't be fooled. It requires deep mastery of the basics, which can only be achieved through dedicated practice, effort and study.

Mastering our song is no different. Who am I? What do I care about? What are my strengths, gifts and talents? My weaknesses, deficits and quirks? What brings me joy and fills me with energy? What do I have a knack for? On the other oft-ignored hand, what drains and exhausts me? Where am I all thumbs? What feels forced in my life? Through the ongoing process of self-discovery, the answers to those deeply universal questions reveal our own unique music. In coming to honestly and intimately know our true selves, we learn to compose the music in the key of our life. To sing our song means to be as fully ourselves as we can in all that we think, say and do. My song hits the air when I speak up by taking a different political stance than the one with which I was raised. Today when I sit in my church that welcomes all, rather than one which closes its doors to difference, the hymn I'm singing is mine. Whether it is putting words on the page or standing on a stage, hiking in the woods or getting lost in a book, gathering people in our home or leading a retreat, coaching a client or stacking wood with my husband, if it is true to who I am, the song is mine. If it isn't, it's not. And so it is with each of us. It is as simple as that and as hard as it gets.

We get good at what we practice. If we rehearse music other than our own, we'll get good at someone else's song. Our song? Well, it just got crossed out, which means that to some degree, our life just got crossed out. A glass of wine momentarily helps us forget that. At least if you happen to be like me, it probably has. More than once. When we try to be who we're not in order to please someone else? Our ~~song.~~ A glass of chardonnay, please. And don't be stingy on that pour. Say what others want to hear to stay in their good graces? Our ~~song.~~ A glass of the House Red, stat! Invest time and energy in someone else's priorities at the ongoing expense of our own? Our ~~song.~~ Lip-syncing someone else's song can send us scurrying to belly up to the wine bar.

Mastering our own song is not a one-and-done thing.

It's a lifelong process, which means we have to choose to just keep showing up and practicing, no matter what. Our music deserves the laser focus and dedication of a world-class musician, because that is what we are. Each in a class of our own, the world is waiting for the song that can only be heard through us. *Songs in the Key of Life*[7] came to be known as the signature album of the Grammy Award winning American singer-song writer Stevie Wonder because it was recognizable and characteristic of his music. It sounded like him. Imagine Stevie Wonder trying to sound like Andrea Bocelli. Or Macklemore. Or Alvin and The Chipmunks. It wouldn't work, everyone would know it, and we'd all miss out. Krista Tippet, host of the NPR radio show "On Being," recently encouraged one of her guests just prior to the start of the interview to "just sound like yourself and you will be brilliant."[8] Only when we sound like ourselves, will the brilliance of our song shine through. The trick then, is tuning our inner ears to our own key, so that we know when we are being true to who we are and when we are not. Sometimes we need help to tell the difference.

My beloved friend Kristine and I once attended a creativity retreat held in Taos, New Mexico. We stayed in a beautiful little inn where creative souls like Georgia O'Keefe, D.H. Lawrence and Martha Graham hung out. The inn was built next to Native American land considered sacred. The first night of the retreat a sheet of paper with the heading Open Mic Night appeared on the door to the dining room. People were giddy to sign up. In our midst were poets and musicians, storytellers and magicians. And then there was us. Participation was optional. We exercised our option – until later that night when we were forced to change our tune. Standing in our room looking out over those sacred hills, it hit me. That still small inner voice showed up and wouldn't be still. Like a conductor tapping her baton, waiting for me to come to attention, she persisted. I tried to ignore her. Until I couldn't.

"Oh fuck," I said out loud.

"What?" Kristine wanted to know.

"We're supposed to sign up for Open Mic Night."

"Doing what???" she asked.

"We're supposed to sing."

"And just what in the hell are we supposed to sing?" she demanded.

"Holy Ground"[9] (a song we both knew from a church we had attended years ago).

"Holy fuck," she said. "You're right."

We went and added our names to the list.

A woman in the workshop was a pianist, and we asked her if she would play for us, hoping that while practice might not make perfect, it could at least make better. The group at this gathering was eclectic, with multiple spiritual traditions represented. Because our song had specific Christian language we decided to substitute a few words so as to not offend anyone, and resonate with everyone. Kind of like Kenny G. Our pianist didn't know the original words to our song, but the second we sang the changed lyrics during our practice session, she stopped playing. "Are those the actual words to the song?" she asked. Whaaat?? How did she pick that up? We told her that we had changed the words to accommodate others. "Well, they don't work and you should sing the words that you know, not change them to try and fit in." That should be a bumper sticker.

Two nights later we climbed up onto the stage, held hands, closed our eyes to avoid any sympathetic looks from the audience, and sang about standing on holy ground. The standing ovation at the end wasn't for our gifted voices. It was for the gift of our song to which we gave voice. When the song is ours, the ground upon which we stand is always holy, because our song isn't a performance. It is an offering.

A performance is something done for the entertainment of others. It is a production meant to wow an audience, win their approval, and warrant their applause. An offering on the other hand, is a gift given for the enrichment of others. It is a contribution meant to benefit another, touch for the good, and bless the recipient. Now, concert pianists and rock stars, stand-up comics and actors, rodeo clowns and professional football players, ballerinas and slam poets all actually perform on some sort of stage. Is theirs a performance or an offering?

Am I performing or offering?

What about you?

That's the million-dollar question awaiting our own priceless answer. The world is in need of our gift of song. Without it, there's work that won't get done, people that won't be loved, lives that won't be touched and changes that won't be made. Imagine a world without the songs of Mother Theresa or Lady Gaga, Gloria Steinem or Gabby Giffords, Malala Yousafzai or Misty Copeland, "Rosy the Riveter" or Rosa Parks, Betty Friedan or Betty Ford, Jane Austen or Jane Goodall, Billie Holiday or Billie Jean King, the Virgin Mary or Eve Ensler's Vagina Monologues.

Imagine a world without your song?

My song?

Her song?

A cause for the deepest kind of sorrow.

4

LADIES SING THE BLUES

Does wine really drown our sorrows?

∽

"Avoiding pain, we may linger in the vicinity of our
wounds, sometimes for many years, gathering the
courage to experience them."[10]
RACHEL NAOMI REMEN, M.D.

SOMETIMES A GIRL HAS TO SING THE BLUES. She just
does. There is no getting around it; sorrow is a part of
life. Pain and loss, sadness and grief, disappointment
and failure, wounds and afflictions, hardship and struggle;
all come knocking on our doors. It's what we do with
them that counts. Some of my greatest teachers have
been my hardest lessons. The darkest times have shed
the brightest lights. My highest joy is woven into my
deepest hurt. The greatest accomplishments took root
in my biggest failures. Sadness and pain invite us to
become more fully human, to grow deeper and stronger,

and to develop kindness and compassion for the pain of others. The sorrows I have experienced differ, as have my responses to them. Sticking with my commitment to be curious, I decided to look more deeply at the role wine has played when sorrow and loss were at my doorstep. When did I use wine as a deadbolt, losing the chance to discover what they had to reveal, both in and for me? When did I unlock my interior door and welcome them in as unexpected guests bearing gifts?

The week before our mom died, we all moved into my parents' house. At her side during her last days, moments and breaths, we were given the miraculous gift of walking her home. We sat on the edge of her bed, telling stories that made us laugh, sharing memories that brought us to tears. Angels seemed close and it felt like church, as their home filled with people who came to wish her on her way. It was a time of grace and goodness, pain and sadness. In other words, it was rich. At the end of every evening our friend, Don, came by with his guitar and two bottles of wine. We would toast the end of each precious day and he would sing to her. It felt like a prayer, and those shared glasses of wine were a sacrament. Like the last supper, when we drank that wine, we did it in remembrance of her.

There have been a few times in my life when loss has been so monumental and of such magnitude that it felt like I would never, never, never recover. Ever. When

I was about ten years old, my future sister-in-law, Ursula, came from Germany to visit us for Christmas. Her family had hosted my brother, Peter, when he studied abroad for a year. With her that Christmas was Ara, her daughter born a few years after he came back for his final year at Stanford. That little girl was nothing if not a bundle of joy, and I fell in love immediately. If Peter hadn't asked Ursula to marry him, I would have. Even as a young girl, Ara was an old soul. She seemed to see and understand life more deeply than the rest. When she was about 16, I was out visiting their family farm. My brother had long since adopted Ara as his own, and their family now included a little sister. As I was about to get into my car to leave, having given hugs all around, Ara ran after me for one more. Throwing her arms around my neck, she said, "I love you, Aunt Molly." As I drove away I couldn't get that last hug out of my mind. It felt, final.

I never saw her again. Shortly thereafter, she was struck and killed by a drunk driver.

When I got the phone call the night of the accident, it brought me to my knees, and evoked a deep cry of grief that sounded part wounded animal, part insane asylum. Unexpected loss, coming far too early, is about as excruciatingly raw and extraordinarily real as pain can get. Standing in the church at her funeral, the pews so full that people spilled into the aisle and out the front door, I found that I needed to sit squarely in the middle of the sorrow and mourn. Mourning is what my friend, the poet Ann Staley, describes as "that ancient form of love."[11] In the months and years that followed, as I allowed myself to drink in the sadness and heartache, grief and loss, Ara eventually found a resting place inside. Mending my life back together around her loss, rather than pushing it away, felt like a way to mark her life well, deepening my own inner reservoir in the process. Wine drunk to escape that pain would have prevented me from grieving fully, leaving me ill equipped to be present for the grief of others.

There is a cleansing that takes place when we grieve with our whole hearts. By moving through it, rather than hiding from it, we come out the other side made more whole through our willingness to be broken. To be human is to, at times, find ourselves filled with sorrow and sadness along our way. However, most of us don't tolerate sadness very well and would prefer different traveling companions. Ones like joy and peace, happiness and fun. Now, those sound like the makings for a great road trip. We like fellow travelers who are neat and tidy, like to sing along to the music with the windows rolled down, help pay for the gas, sleep with their mouths closed and stay on our carefully planned schedule. We have places to go, people to see and things to do. But sorrow is a mess. She's a chain smoker and wouldn't crack a window if you paid her. She inhales deeply and our lungs fill with her smoke. She's broke so any fuel for the trip is on us. Sorrow is so tired that her half-eaten sandwich falls on the floor, and she needs to stop and spend the night in a roadside motel. She likes to fall asleep to Billie Holiday, snores like a sailor so we find it almost impossible to get any sleep, and her timetable is her own. She doesn't mean to stay forever, but she won't be rushed, and like a hitchhiker, she is dependent on the kindness of strangers. She is in our car and we are her ride to the next stop along her way. Oh, and don't even think about pulling out a bottle of wine, or she will stick around even longer. She is a founding member of MADD and will remind you that drinking and driving don't mix, and well, friends don't let friends drive drunk.

Whether we want to admit it or not, for this leg of the trip, she is our companion, dare I say it, even our friend. The quicker we are able to take hold of her extended hand of friendship, slow down, tend to her gently and listen to her sad tale, the sooner she will see that her job here is done. In the meantime, feed her well, make sure she has plenty of blankets against the chill that seems to permeate her bones, take side-trips to hidden sights that only she knows, go for evening walks even if it is raining, run her a hot bath and give her a journal. Sometimes she's too tired to speak. She'll leave the journal behind because she likes to travel light. Others will pick her up along her way, but in the meantime, she is ours. It's when we try and push her out of our moving car that we get into trouble, because we'll just find her waiting for us around the next bend. We don't realize that she, along with all of the shadowy emotions we'd rather not feel, is here to guide, heal and teach us more about our common humanity; more about who we are and what we care about. She is, as Rumi says in his poem, The Guest House, "Sent as a guide from beyond."[12] If we take the time, we might even notice that once sorrow has moved on, there is more room in our car for joy, peace, happiness and fun than there was even before she came.

Sorrow may be a part of our shared journey, but I don't believe she is meant to be the destination. There are expected losses that most of us can count on. Losing a parent. Children growing up. Jobs that come to an end. Plans that don't pan out. Years that tick by too fast. The girl in the mirror that now looks strangely like your mother. Some of these seemed easier to navigate than others, and then, there was the year that I have come to call simply "Good-bye."

My mom passed in June.

Two daughters left for college in September.

The two younger ones disappeared into high school.

Dad, without Mom, couldn't die fast enough.

Since that didn't seem to be quite enough to handle, we put our house on the market two months after he was gone.

All I did was wave goodbye, cry, get a therapist and start on an anti-depressant.

Lost parents.

Emptying nest.

Lost nest.

Different nest.

On top of that I was in the throes of menopause, which meant that I was losing my waistline, my sleep, my neck and my mind. I was just all kinds of fun.

Sorrow is defined as "a feeling of sadness or grief caused especially by the loss of someone or something"[13] The sorrow I seek to avoid by drinking wine seems connected to the loss of my song, some aspect of my self. Whether it is my voice or my passions, my beliefs or my time, my body or my values, any time I give up a bit of my self, sorrow follows, and a glass of wine starts to sound really good. Two? Even better. Like the time I sold my horses.

For as long as I can remember, if it neighed, I loved it. I bought my first horse when I was 12. A few years later she gave birth and my stable grew to two. My summers growing up were spent working as a wrangler on a guest ranch, and during the school year I spent every spare minute with my two four-footed friends. When it came time to buy my first car, nothing but a Ford Mustang would do. A '65, it was shiny white outside with red leather inside. I had scrimped and saved to buy all of my horses, and whether driving down the road or riding up the trail, I was whistling a happy tune. At 22, when I married my first husband, I still owned all of my horses. Until one day when I came home to find the mustang gone, and in its parking space a brand new lemon-yellow van in the driveway. The kind with no windows favored by kidnappers and drug dealers. Apparently, "we" had made the decision to sell the one and buy the other. As I saw it, we had discussed…not decided. I was furious, hurt, and resentful. I was also afraid, intimidated and reluctant to speak up due to our invisible roommate named Anger. Rather than stand up for myself, I swallowed my feelings along with a few glasses of wine. Not long after, because we needed the money, I sold my horses, put away my cowboy boots, hung up my saddle, and poured some more wine. The money was a drop in the bucket. Selling what I loved? Priceless. When I sold those horses, some of my song left with them. We pay a tall price when we sell ourselves short. The moral of the story? Hold [on to] your horses.

Wine can be a means of escaping pain, numbing the ache, dulling the jagged edges of loneliness, ignoring issues that need resolving and wounds in need of healing. Do we see sorrow and pain as in invitation to, or a retreat from? Is wine just a kind of exit strategy? For those of us who have tried that, a few too many glasses of wine can cloud almost any stark reality that begs for our clear-headed attention. The next morning after the fog of wine has worn off, that pain, those aches, that loneliness and those realities are still there. In the light of day it turns out that, yes, money really is that tight, a daughter really is that unhappy, no, we actually haven't dealt with our family-of-origin shit, yes, our marriage is in deep trouble, our work schedule really is that empty, or we actually do have to get on an airplane again, and yes, our work is so unfulfilling that we dread getting out of bed in the morning. Barbara Brown Taylor, in her book *Learning to Walk in the Dark*, says that she "learned that sadness does not sink a person; it is the energy a person spends trying to avoid sadness that does that."[14]

Drowning our sorrows in wine is a cute way of saying that we drink wine to forget our heartaches and problems. Doing that over and over is about as helpful as going to the dentist for a toothache and getting anesthetized, but never having the root canal. In the morning the tooth still aches.

5

THERE'S A HOLE IN MY BUCKET

Are we drowning in expectations?

～

"Women hold up half the sky."
CHINESE PROVERB

HOW CAN I PUT THIS DELICATELY? If you're a woman, life is a cluster-fuck. There are expectations around almost every aspect of our lives. We are to lean in, stand out, speak up, pay our dues, do what it takes, take it like a man, be assertive but not bitchy. Dress for success, keep up with our friends, and make time for ourselves. Raise our kids and care for our parents. Keep an organized home. In a Pottery Barn kind of way. Have an adventurous and lively sex life, and not let a commitment to a family bed, exhaustion or arthritic knees get in our way. The list is endless and could drive a Mormon woman to drink. And probably has.

How can we hold onto our songs in the midst of

such complicated lives? We have multiple hats to wear, balls to juggle and pieces to hold together. Knowing which hat to wear, and when, gets confusing. Juggling too many balls takes our eye off our own. Keeping it all together, we eventually come apart at the seams. Holding up too much of the sky, the ground crumbles under our feet. With the weight of the very real needs that press upon us, the expectations of others that we adopt as our own, and the relentless internal expectations we set for ourselves, it feels impossible to carry anything, much less our own tune. Our song drains away in our attempts to appear to effortlessly hold everything not only up, but together. Wine helps maintain the image.

A woman with a glass of wine looks for all the world like she has her shit together. There's an air of sophistication about it. It's only wine for crying out loud. It isn't like we are downing martinis or swilling vodka when no one is around. With wine we don't have to drink alone behind closed doors. Well, maybe every now and then. Like when your brother starts quoting the gospel according to Rush Limbaugh at a family gathering. Or your dinner guests have the nerve to accept your invitation to linger awhile longer. Can't they see you were just being polite? Or after hanging up the phone having said yes to yet another commitment, because we didn't want to disappoint "them." We hide our wine in plain sight, drinking from lovely glasses for all to see. It helps us look the part, even if inside we are falling apart because we can't meet all of those expectations, and have lost sight of our own lives. Gripping our wine glass like a life raft, we don't even notice that we are drowning in the Sea of Great Expectations. Like dear Henry, there's a hole in our bucket, but we're too busy bailing out other boats to fix it.

An expectation is a strongly held belief that something should or will happen, be accomplished or achieved. Whose expectations are we meeting? What to-do list are we checking off? Whose priorities are we tending to? Whose projects are we finishing? What standards of success are we striving for? Why do we take on expectations without question? To be loved and valued? Check. Feel worthy? Check. Justify our real estate on the planet? Check. Have a sense of worth and belonging? Check. Avoid having to think about things we'd rather not, like whatever it is that wakes us up at 3AM? Check! Check!

Our own expectations and priorities get so muddled with those of other's, including the people we care about the most, those of the media, and of our culture, that straining our own out of the muddied water feels near impossible. When we feel like we never measure up (and how can we with all of those under-met expectations pouring into our leaky bucket?), it is easy to look for any means to forget how short we are falling from "the" mark. Wine can do the trick. Until the next morning when we wake up and do it all again. Like Bill Murray in the comedy, *Groundhog Day*[15], we are caught in our own time loop. Only, it isn't funny. And we will stay caught in that loop until we stop, take stock, and re-examine things with a clear head.

Gathering un-examined expectations is a lot like filling up our own garage. My dear friend talks about a moment of realization when one day, opening the door to their garage, it hit her. Where had all of that stuff come from? A light bulb went on in her head as she realized that the accumulation of that stuff occurred ever so slowly and just one thing at a time A soccer ball here, an extra suitcase there, boxes of old photographs, kids' art projects, tax returns, chairs in need of mending, half-used cans of paint, spare parts to some gadget or machine that we might need some day. We accumulate until one day there is no room in our 3-car garage for a bicycle. The same is true of the expectations we gather, rarely finding time to stop and evaluate: Is this mine or not? We just do. And try. And pretend. And keep quiet. Until one day there is no room in our own life for us, and we don't even know how or when it happened. Like Mr. Darcy in Jane Austen's *Pride and Prejudice*, we "… cannot fix on the hour or the spot, or the look or the words, which laid the foundation."[16] While he was talking about his love for Elizabeth, the question for us is, when did our own need to meet all these accumulated expectations begin?

Expectations for how life should turn out usually start pretty early. What to think. Who to be. How to be. What to do. In my case, it was a given that I would go to college, and I would get married. Being a girl, my parents saw the former as a means to the latter, and because I was too young to have figured myself out, I couldn't yet challenge their way of thinking by coming up with my own. Getting to college in the first place meant surviving high school. Smart, shy, tall and awkward, I did everything I could to fly under the dangerous teenage radar screen. Expected to fit in and aware that I didn't, I kept my head down in the halls, and my mouth shut in class, even though I almost always had something good to say. I hung out along the wall at school dances with the other flowers. One time, in a flash of temporary insanity, I walked right up to a table filled with the in-crowd at lunch, and as if under the spell of momentary Tourette's, asked the boy I secretly had a crush on to go to the Sadie Hawkins dance with me. While he was the stuff of my dreams, the deafening silence and stares of disbelief woke me up to the fact that this was my worst nightmare. He had no clue who I was, nor did he want to. It was like that dream where you find yourself locked out of the house with no clothes on. Thank God I remembered to get dressed that morning.

Thankfully, college was different. Professors listened when I spoke, answered my questions thoughtfully, and other students paid attention to my ideas. Falling deeply in love with learning, and learning to love myself, I started to hear the faint melody of a song that sounded like mine. Humming it led to singing, as I began to set new expectations for myself. Daring ones. Powerful ones. A master's degree appeared on the horizon when a favorite professor encouraged me to consider graduate school, offering to introduce me to the department chair at a university that would be a great fit. One day that same professor pulled me aside after class, "Would you teach a class for me this week when I have to be out of town?" Would I? Yes! Yes! Hell yes! His expectation was that I would. Mine was that I actually could. Racing back to my room to start preparing, I felt like Maria in the *Sound of Music*[17], singing from the mountaintops, and I couldn't wait to tell someone. Who better than my dad? (Almost anyone as it turned out.) Grabbing the phone, I dialed home, shared the good news and waited for the standing ovation that never came. The phone stayed quiet for Way. Too. Long. "Molly, you have to be careful not to appear too smart or you will intimidate the boys in the class." His words took my breath away. Literally.

Gathering my courage and standing up as tall as I could, I said, "Thanks Dad. I'll keep that in mind. Now

I have to go get ready to teach that class."

I hung up the phone.

Taught the class.

Graduated magna cum laude a year later.

Went on to graduate school and continued to teach, inspire, and of course, intimidate some men along the way.

And married the smart, kind, strong, handsome med-school bound football player who loved me for my brain and my own brand of beauty.

I wish.

That is the song I wish I'd had the courage to sing. Mine were the expectations I wish I had set out to meet. Instead, as my dad's words hung in the air, my first thought was, "But I am smart. If I can't be that, what am I?" Hanging up the phone the only voice I could hear was his, the only expectations to be met were his, the only approval to earn was his. In his defense, he thought he was being helpful. Patriarchal and protective, my best shot at happiness was to find a husband who could take care of me so that I wouldn't have to worry my pretty little head about things like graduate school, a career and financial independence. His expectation was that I should be well taken care of, not that I could take care of myself. I made another phone call. To the professor. I told him I was sorry but I wouldn't be able to teach the class after all.

I hung up the phone.

Graduated magna cum laude a year later.

Stuck the diploma in a file cabinet somewhere.

Took a job that paid the bills.

And married the first guy who asked.

When we lose our song, we lose access to our inner GPS. Wandering off of our own navigational maps, we get lost. Sometimes for a very long time. A familiar nightly glass of wine or three can lull us into a false sense of security. But in the morning, we're still lost.

6

JUST THE WAY YOU AREN'T

Why do we strive for impossible perfection?

❧

"One of the most radical things women can do is to
love their body."[18]

E V E   E N S L E R

IF THERE IS A WOMAN WHO HAS NEVER struggled with
body image, I haven't met her yet. The chances that my
reflection in the bathroom mirror ever measures up to
some illusive standard I seem to have set for myself are
slim to none. And, don't even think about getting me
started on selfies. My arm will never be long enough. In
the search for a better body, I stand in front of the mirror,
suck in my tummy, pull up my thighs trying to see if I
still have knee caps, and take what used to be tight on a
short hike up my hill, only to have gravity pull it back
down. I still like my arms and shoulders, but even they
are threatening mutiny. Rather than look in the mirror

and love who we see, most of us turn away, discouraged with our imperfect bodies. Recently, I was trying on a new pair of jeans in a dressing room, and at the top of the mirror, in lovely letters was written, "Use Kind Words." I can't remember the last time I used kind words when talking about my body. Can you? I once worked with a wonderful masseuse who, as she rubbed and kneaded away, quietly said things like, "Such good legs. You work so hard for her. Thank you for all you do to support her." Now those are some kinda kind words.

The standards to which we compare ourselves are the images that smile at us from every screen, billboard, runway and glossy page. And the teeth that are smiling are, of course, blindingly white. The magic of Photoshop can erase every furrow, wrinkle and line that we have ever earned. It is the rare day that I, along with most of the women I know, don't look in the mirror, place our hands lightly on either side of our face, and pull up and back ever so slightly. "Just a little tweak," we say. A little lift here, a touch of Botox there, a smidgen of filler around the lips, a wee nip and tuck to give us our necks back. I am always on the lookout for the perfect black cashmere sweater, preferably one with a turtleneck to cover up what used to be my neck. When talking with a younger woman, it is hard to concentrate on what she is saying because I'm so distracted by her perfect jawline, envious that she still has one. Cosmetic treatments are on the rise, and any way you slice it, the message is that who we are is not enough. In a culture that holds impossible standards of beauty so dear, we pay dearly when we can't measure up. A bottle of wine is so much easier to find and cheaper to buy than the fountain of youth promised by a multi-billion dollar industry.

When did it become not okay to age? Or even more to the point, when did it become okay not to age? Measuring who we are with who we think we should be, comparing ourselves to images that aren't even real, we strive for the impossible. Years ago, Jamie Lee Curtis agreed to have herself photographed without the magic eraser of technology.[19] The images of her photo-edited self were presented side-by-side with the ones of the 'real' her. It was a courageous, gracious and liberating act. It was like looking at Barbie standing next to a real girl, who if she were real, wouldn't be able to stand on her own two adorable little high-heeled feet. She'd topple over on her perfect little plastic nose.

After my divorce in my late 30s, I found myself single and playing the dating game again for the first time in years. All the insecurities of adolescence came roaring back. Would anyone find me even remotely attractive, much less sexy? Pushing out two babies and nursing had taken their normal toll. What I wouldn't give for a pair of perfect breasts. On a tight budget, raising my girls on my own, breast implants were out of sight. Until I got that tax refund. What better way to use it? I could figure out saving for college, buying a house, starting that emergency fund and getting new tires for the car later. I cashed the check and made an appointment with a cosmetic surgeon, who if he hadn't gone to medical school would have sold fancy cars for a living. He oozed slickness in his high priced office and alligator cowboy boots. "You're gonna love the new you." Which of course meant that the 'old' me didn't cut it. "How about when I actually am older?" I wondered aloud. "How will they hold up over the years?" He winked, flashing his pearly whites. "Honey, you'll have the best tits in the nursing home." Great. Nothing like perky tits when shuffling down to dinner in my walker.

Standing back in front of the mirror in my new bikini, checking out my new $3,000 breasts, I was pretty sure the surgeon had made a mistake. He must have grabbed the wrong set off the shelf. It was midnight and I kept turning this way and that in front of my full-length mirror, feeling like Goldilocks might have felt if the three bears had only had two beds. My new breasts were definitely not "just right." They weren't big enough, high enough, or round enough. They weren't "enough" enough. A glass of wine eased the disappointment. After two, I was starting to think I looked pretty hot. A third, and I decided I was ready to take them for a test drive. The next day I joined a dating service. I had met my first husband in a bar, and this new strategy felt like a major step up. As it turned out, I was still looking for love in all the wrong places.

What in the world had I been thinking when I decided to get my implants? Nothing. I hadn't been thinking but comparing. In striving to be who we are not, we lose who we are. Constant comparison to impossible perfection can only lead to sorrow. Maybe we drink wine to comfort us in our sadness and frustration over losing ourselves in the search of a different self. A better self. I don't know what anyone else needs to do to feel good when they look in the mirror, and it might sound like I am against any and all plastic surgery or cosmetic treatments. Obviously, I'm not. There are times when it is exactly what a woman needs in order to feel comfortable in her own skin. I am, however, against an industry and a culture that tells me to go out and buy the "right" skin.

Recently I worked with a personal trainer. She asked about my goals for our work together. Lose weight? Build muscle? A bikini-ready body? I thought for a minute and then said, "I want to find the body that is mine." There was a powerful feeling of freedom in that answer. Sort of like taking off a pair of spanx. At 60 years old, I wanted to know what it felt like to be me at my own best. Strong, healthy and as fit as I could muster. We got to work, and once I quit trying to have someone else's body, I began to appreciate my own.

Our bodies matter. We are our own most valuable resource and owe it to ourselves to care for what we've been given. Feed and water it well. Keep it moving. Give it a rest. How we feel about our bodies matters too. Trying to practice using kind words, I actually wrote a few out and put them on my mirror: "I love it that when I look in the mirror, I love who I see." At first that was a bald-faced lie, served up with a hefty helping of fine lines and wrinkles. Come to think of it though, it couldn't be a bald-faced anything or I wouldn't need to have my lip and chin waxed on a regular basis, and never leave the house without a set of tweezers. As false as those words sounded, much less felt in the beginning, I returned to that statement every day, looking in the mirror and repeating them, out loud, to myself. Slowly the lie evolved into acceptance. Acceptance found its way to truth. And the truth, more days than not, sets me free. Or at least free-ish. Looking for love in all the right places begins with the woman in the mirror.

Several years after having them put in, I decided to have my implants removed. The warnings about the dangers of silicone trumped my desire to fill out a bigger bra. Tom came with me to the exploratory meeting with the doctor. He had married me with them in and would love me when they were out. He wanted me healthy, not perfect. During that initial consult, the surgeon, a woman who radiated the perfect mix of confidence and compassion, took one look under my gown and with a twinkle in her eye said, "Honey, what were you thinking? Look at you. You're an athlete! You are going to feel so much better when you are back to your old self." Nursing home be damned. Guess I'll be a saggy shuffler.

Self-acceptance and love are deeply personal experiences. I am for doing what it takes to find contentment with who we are. One size absolutely does not fit all. To fall in love with ourselves in our unique one-of-a-kind perfect imperfection is about as thirst quenching as it gets. Wine doesn't even come close.

A few weeks after the surgery to remove those implants, my girls were snuggled up against me on the couch one evening. Hugging me, one of them sleepily said, "Mama, you feel like you again." Out of the mouth of babes.

7

MAMA SAID THERE'D BE DAZE LIKE THIS

Why do we moms love our wine?

⌒

"When a child comes out of your body, it arrives with about a fifth of your brain clutched in its little hand."[20]

ANNE LAMOTT

FROM THE GET-GO, MOTHERHOOD is complicated by the expectations of what it *should* look like. "I'm expecting" means oh-so-much-more than a baby. Life is suddenly pregnant with new possibilities and old fears, high hopes and low energy, exciting dreams and daunting questions. Societal pressures to have children, or even want them in the first place are all too familiar. The expectations for what it means to be not just a mom, but the right kind of mom, a GOOD mom, come from every direction, including parents, grandparents, friends, "experts" and of course, complete strangers. Those who offer their super helpful advice when your toddler is in the midst of a meltdown in the grocery store aisle, or as your baby is screaming on your lap in the middle seat of the last row of a sold-out red-eye flight tempt even a pacifist to sign up for a concealed weapons class. Parenting advice is stitched on pillows, printed on bumper stickers, touted in books, blogs and parenting magazines. There is the Farmer's Almanac version that says we are to give them roots and wings. It's hard to know which to do when. Kahalil Gibran, (who never had any children of his own) supposedly said, "If you love somebody, let them go…,"[21] which feels about as natural as patting your tummy and rubbing your head. Backwards. While riding a unicycle. But my personal favorite, hands down, is that children are a gift from God. Absolutely. I couldn't agree more. Most days I wanted to send God a lovely, heartfelt, handwritten thank-you note for the best gifts ever. Except for the days when I fantasized how to re-gift them without getting arrested. More times than not, we learn what we need to know after we've already done it, and waste time thinking, "if I only knew then what I know now." Too late. We're already lost in unfamiliar territory, surrounded by new dangers and perils at every turn. Add the external pressure to get it right to the internal pressure to live up to our own self-imposed parenting standards, and there are more than enough reasons to reach for the nearest glass of wine.

I wouldn't trade being a mom for anything, even though it often felt like it took everything. The truth is, since I didn't grow up with dreams of being a mommy, it simply took me completely by surprise. I had one doll when I was little, didn't play with her or give her a name, and gave her away to my mom one Christmas when I realized I'd forgotten to buy a present. Dressed in my Christmas nightie, dragging little No-Name by her hair, I shoved her into my mom's lap as we sat gathered around the tree, and never thought of her again. While other little girls played house, I messed around in my tree fort. They dressed up in aprons and pretended to be mommies, while I donned a baseball uniform with the cap low to cover my curls and sold candy for my cousin's Little League Team. I babysat. Once. Motherhood was just never on my radar screen. Until I gave birth to my daughters. Then it became my only radar screen.

No matter how you romanticize it, it's hard to live in the Mother-hood. Guilt and shame are close neighbors, always peering through our inner windows. Most of us experienced things growing up that we are determined not to repeat with our own children, as in the "by God I'll never spank my children" kind of way. Until we have them, and want to thrash them to within an inch of their precious little lives. More than once. Working moms worry that they are selling their kids short. Stay-at-home moms wonder if they're getting the short end of the stick. Single moms have double the work. Married moms? You do the math. While there's no one right way to do it, it sure as hell feels like there is and you are the only one who hasn't figured it out yet. When you look around, it looks like everyone else has it nailed down, buttoned up and stitched together. And you? You are still searching for the needle and thread. No doubt about it, you are Odd-Mom-Out.

There were so many times that I felt like I didn't measure up on the Mama-meter; calibrated to detect where I fell in relation to the articles in parenting magazine, sitcoms that resolved every parenting issue in under an hour, and stories told by those moms that everyone publicly admires, but secretly hates. The ones who have all their photos in beautiful chronological albums, annual holiday cards with perfect family pictures, manicured nails that never chip, and who fit back into their jeans the week after they give birth. They even pretend that they don't eat cheerios off the floor when every mom knows it is faster than getting out the vacuum. A clean house and some dietary fiber all in one swoop.

One time I attended a fancy schmancy mother-daughter tea party when my girls were still too young to care. Volunteering to be a table hostess meant that I decorated the table and invited others to join me. On a shoestring budget, I borrowed a linen tablecloth from my mom, polished the spots off my best stainless, cleaned the smudges off my votive candle holders, and splurged on two bunches of tulips. Looking around at the other tables, it was obvious that they were hosted by moms who not only had a budget for shoestrings, but for an entire closet full of designer shoes as well. Their tables overflowed with huge bouquets of flowers, ornate china, candelabras, and silverware made out of, well, silver. Desperate to crawl under my table, and open the bottle of wine I hoped I'd find chilling there, but determined to make the best of it and my daughters proud, I plopped my tulips in a mason jar. As if on cue to expose me as a fraud-mommy, every single tulip petal fell off of their stem. Ready to burst into tears and run from the room, my own mom came to my rescue. "Honey, we'll just whimsically scatter them all around the table."

We did.

It didn't help.

Motherhood is a two-sided coin, and everyday a new toss of the coin. Heads? It's amazing, miraculous, fun, enriching, powerful, magical and wonderful. Tails? It's boring, humdrum, colored with resentment and loneliness, not to mention feeling invisible, undervalued, unappreciated and exhausted. Ask any mom (except those ones that we hate, mentioned above) and she will tell you that she totally understands why sleep deprivation is a form of torture used to extract information from prisoners. I once heard of a mom who sprinkled cheerios in the crib around her toddlers at night after they had fallen asleep, in the hopes of catching another wink for herself the next morning. Some nights, trying to rock little ones to sleep looks a little like a martini...more shaken than stirred.

Back when my girls were growing up, almost every mom I knew drank wine. Almost every night. After a day of changing diapers, a glass or two of wine is a change of scenery. Singing Itsy-Bitsy-Spider a hundred and twenty-three times sounds a lot like a drinking song for moms. Picking up the same toys, again, is less boring once we've picked up that lovely glass of wine. Waiting for someone to toast our supermom efforts isn't worth the wait, so why not toast ourselves with a couple of glasses before falling into bed for another night of interrupted sleep. Feeling invisible and undervalued is easier with a little wine under our belts. Except we don't have on a belt, but pants with a drawstring or elastic band. Wine makes us feel a little better about that too.

Mothers can tell you that evenings are the hardest (There's a reason it's called "wine-o'clock"). The kids are tired and cranky. The house is a mess. You are tired and cranky. You feel like a mess and probably look like one too. Your husband is tired and cranky. He usually doesn't look like a mess, which makes you feel worse.

And then he wants to have sex, and you don't. So you feel even worse. From 5PM until bedtime, all you can think about is how ready you are for the day to be over. Seriously. That is how it is. But no one tells you that ahead of time. Back in the day, we moms didn't talk about it with each other either, because we felt so guilty for feeling that way. We loved our kids! We cherished our kids! We were so thankful to have them and couldn't imagine life without them! We just never imagined it could be so hard. Drinking wine just became part of our mom routine. On especially difficult nights, we might quietly pour another glass of wine when no one was looking. The honest to goodness truth about my own experience with wine and motherhood? Wine was like my Mother's Helper, hired to help me through the day. Knowing that I had a glass (or more) waiting for me at the end of the day, which usually felt exactly like the day before, was a thought that kept me going during the mid-afternoon slump. Once that glass of wine was poured, everything felt a little easier.

Being a mom is kind of like living in an eternal labor and delivery room. The labor pains come in waves as we birth them into their next phase. And the next and the next and the next. Over the years wine was my anesthetic of choice. Giving birth and those first few days however, should have been a clue to the cause one signs up for when becoming a mom. A labor of love if ever there was one, I thought I knew what the word love meant, until that exact moment when I held my newborn daughter for the first time. I'd never known a love like that, and in that instant I knew that I would do whatever it took to protect and take care of that little girl. No. Matter. What. I would give up my last drop of blood for her, and almost did during delivery, requiring an infusion of several pints of blood. Being a mom takes everything you've got, and plenty of what you don't. Sometimes the pain is so intense that it feels like you will never recover. In the next moment, the joy and love are so over the moon that it feels like you may never return to earth.

The night after Haley was born was like a bad Hitchcock film meets *One Flew Over The Cuckoo's Nest*.[22] There was a tremendous storm. The wind howled, windows shook, rain came down in torrents, pelting against the shaking windows, and finally, the power in the hospital went out. All of our beds were rolled out into the hallway. Rooms were dark and the hospital was running on generator power. Women in various stages of labor were moaning, others were snoring, and still others were creeping their way down the hall to the bathroom.

While we are on the subject of bathrooms, in case you didn't know this fun tidbit, along with delivering a baby, in order to go home with them, you have to deliver something else. If I didn't want to raise my daughter in the bowels of the hospital, I had to prove I could still move my own. Kicked out of our rooms by the storm, we were all sharing one bathroom. This has never been my strong suit, and the word "clench" comes to mind. Still, the nurses had been very clear on this one little point. Every visit for the past 8 hours started with, "Honey, have you had a bowel movement yet?" Yet? I was sure I would never have one again. Ever. Until the moment that I knew I had to. Now.

It was still dark, so I asked the nice nurse nearby to kindly direct me to the bathroom. She pointed down the hallway and said it was on my left. Clenching for all I was worth, I waddled my way towards the bathroom. Clench. Waddle. Waddle. Clench. Where the hell was that bathroom? A door on my left looked promising. Opening it I stepped inside, and in the dim light could see that I was actually in the cleaning and supply closet. Brooms, mops, paper towels, cleaning supplies. Shit! Exactly! It was now or never. Babies aren't the only things to "crown" on their way out. I forgot to mention there was one other thing in that broom closet: One of those nifty wheelchairs with a bedpan in it. My apologies to whomever found that wheelchair the next morning. You will definitely get your own bathroom in heaven.

Rudyard Kipling said, "God could not be every-where, and therefore he made mothers."[23] Seriously? Leave it to a man to say that. It sounds kind of like God is off on vacation, and we're left minding the store. Except we are all-alone and can't find the instruction manual. What makes motherhood so tricky is that much of the time what is required goes completely against our grain. Babies are born utterly and completely helpless, dependent on us in every way in order to survive. Serving as their protector and caretaker feels as natural as breathing. In order to thrive however, they have to learn to help themselves and become independent. It is in the midst of their struggles that they learn to take hold of their own lives and make their own way. Literally and figuratively, they are meant to fall down, get hurt, dust themselves off, lick their wounds, get up and go at it again. And again. And again.

Shame and vulnerability expert, Brené Brown, says that as human beings we arrive on the planet hardwired for struggle.[24] I hate that she is right, and her just a tiny bit for saying it. Think of the butterfly. Encased in the cocoon, the struggle to get out is what gives the emerging insect the wing strength to fly. If a well-meaning observer tries to help make it easier by peeling away the outer layer, the butterfly never takes flight. The same is true for our children. Yet standing by as they flounder and fall, get hurt and give up, take wrong turns and dangerous detours feels a lot like cutting off our own arm. With a dull knife.

Sometimes I couldn't do it and made it worse by

peeling away a few layers of their cocoon, making it harder for them to find their own wings. Like paying for all of their auto insurance, gas and repair bills during high school. And beyond. We didn't want them to have to go to school, play sports AND get a job for goodness sakes. At one time we owned six cars so they wouldn't have to share and could easily make it to all of their various activities. That was the year our mechanic sent us a thank-you card for being their best customer. Making it a little harder on our children earlier might have made it a lot easier for them later.

Step-parenting is a high calling, and takes motherhood up a notch. Learning what it takes is usually more error than trial. When Tom and I got married I was blessed with his two daughters, Clare and Val. I wouldn't trade those beauties for anything. To say that I adore them both is an understatement. At the time we all got together, all four girls were climbing the steps of puberty, while I was sliding down the slippery slopes of Mt. Menopause. My volcano-studying husband used to pray for an eruption, just to get out of the molten lava flow of estrogen that surged through our home. More than a few issues often found us on different sides of our family tree. Literally.

Every Christmas we would go out in search of the perfect evergreen. Tromping from tree to tree to tree we inevitably split along family lines. Me and my two on one side, Tom and his two on the other. It always ended in tears, as we dragged another imperfect tree back to the car. We knew about "yours" and "mine," but struggled mightily to figure out what was meant by "ours." We came together under one roof with lots of love and the best of intentions, and tried to "blend". (Whoever came up with that term should have tried harder.) In trying to do it right, I often I got it wrong. Trying to be "fair" often meant that someone felt short-changed. I loved my husband's daughters deeply but differently than my own, and try as I might, I knew that I couldn't make up for what they'd lost when their family broke apart. At night, all I could think of to do was light the candles as dinner cooked on the stove, and pour another glass of wine.

Motherhood feels like an impossible dance. Hold on. Let go. Stand firm. Give in. Speak up. Pipe down. Close our mouths. Open our ears. Lend a hand. Let them handle it. Lock the doors. Open the gates. Like the hokey-pokey, the only thing to do is put your whole self in and shake it all around. That is what living in the mother-hood is all about. The dance goes on even as they are adults, living their own lives. While I am grateful for the deep roots and strong wings each has developed, I still hate it when they are in pain, face tough challenges or are unhappy, as much as I ever did. To this day when I answer a phone call from one of our daughters, I am filled with both thrill and trepidation. Do they want to go shoe shopping together, or has the other shoe dropped? Whoever first said that "we are only as happy as our unhappiest child" knew a thing or two about parenting.

It boils down to this: Being a mom doesn't look anything like you expect it to. All the flowers drop off their stems, and you do your best to whimsically scatter them about. The power goes out. The wind blows. You lose a lot of blood. You go looking for a bathroom and find a broom closet. And yet, for me, when it comes to striking it rich in the precious metal of meaning, nothing compares to the mother lode, mined smack dab in the middle of the Mother-hood. And yet, the sheer mettle required to carry the mother-load often led to one too many glasses of wine at night, which felt a lot like those pints of blood after yet another day of labor and delivery. But of course, it wasn't.

It is interesting to note that while both of my daughters enjoy an alcoholic beverage, neither particularly enjoys wine. Maybe observing me gave wine a bad taste in their mouths. Thankfully, when I told them about writing this book, they didn't say, "It's about time, Mom." But they also didn't say, "I have no idea what you are talking about." They knew me with a glass of wine in my hand in the evening, and the smell of it on my breath as I read to them before bed. I didn't feel great about it back then, but when I looked around, other moms were doing the same thing. I don't feel great about it now either, but it is too late to do anything about the past, except share my own experience as a cautionary tale. I wonder what we moms miss out on by drinking a little too much wine? A missed conversation with an adolescent at a crucial time? A molten moment? A missed memory? The chance to avoid an unchangeable regret? While I'll never know what I missed, I hope that as moms, my daughters will never have to wonder the same thing.

8

(WO)MEN AT WORK

Why does work drive us to wine?

∽

"If you want something said, ask a man; if you want
something done, ask a woman."[25]

MARGARET THATCHER

TO WORK OR NOT TO WORK? That isn't really the question since, according to the US Department of Labor, women make up about 47% of the labor force.[26] Of those, over 74% work full-time[27], and approximately 70% of women with children under the age of 18 are actively employed.[28] Findings published by the Pew Research Center indicate that 40% of all homes with children under the age of 18 include mothers who are either the sole or primary breadwinners.[29] Depending on the source, the median income of women today hovers slightly above or below 80% of that of our male counterparts and, wait for it...we are still responsible for a disproportionate share of childcare and household responsibilities (even though COO of Facebook and co-author of *Lean In: Women, Work, and the Will to Lead*, Sheryl Sandberg, says that the data show men who participate equally in domestic responsibilities – loosely paraphrasing here – get laid more often[30]... just sayin').

In her 2015 TED-x talk, Jessica Shortfall, author of *Work. Pump. Repeat: The New Mom's Guide to Breastfeeding and Going Back To Work*, states that 23% of women return to work just two weeks after giving birth. According to Shortfall, this is due to the lack of access to paid maternity leave experienced by a staggering 88% of women in America. Along with only a preemie's fistful of countries in the world, including such powerhouse economies as Papua New Guinea, Suriname and the tiny island nations of Micronesia, Marshall Islands, Nauru, Niue, Palau and Tonga, the US does not offer any level of national paid leave to new mothers. You might be thinking, at least these new moms have access to unpaid leave right? Not so fast Ms. Shortfall says. Due to the way it is structured and numerous exceptions, less than half of new mothers are eligible for FMLA (Family Medical Leave Act). [31]

One final wrinkle is the added responsibility of caring for aging parents. According to the Family Caregiver Alliance, approximately 66% of caregivers are female, the average caregiver being a 49-year-old married, employed woman caring for her mother who does not live with her. While men do participate in such care, women are likely to spend as much as 50% more time on their care-giving responsibilities.[32] And, none of these data reflect the growing numbers of those in the "sandwich generation" who take care of young children, a parent or two at the same time, often while attempting to meet the usual financial and life obligations of other adults in their 30s and 40s. Those in their 50s and 60s are often continuing to help out their adult children through financial assistance, living space and caring for grandchildren, while still caring for their own aging parents. Is it any wonder that this is a "sandwich" often washed down with a few glasses of wine?

Statistics-schmatistics. Who needs studies and data to tell us the long and short of it? We are working more than ever, on fewer hours of sleep, and for less money than the opposite sex. Workingwomen are leaving their babies in the care of someone else earlier than ever before, and caring for aging parents longer than they ever imagined. For the majority of us working girls, our work doesn't end when we finally close our office door for the day. The end of one job is merely the beginning of another. Anyone else ready for a glass of wine yet?

Numbers may shine a bright light on some of the pressures working women face, however, they leave other factors lurking in our shadows. Tiny things like job satisfaction, increasing expectations with decreasing resources, an increasingly competitive work environment, not to mention the pressures to have and do it all while making it all look easy. For workingwomen, chasing the American dream can feel more like a nightmare. Granted, some of us enjoy what we do, love what we do, are great at what we do, and will do almost anything to keep doing it. But it's a safe assumption that few of us can work for the sheer pleasure of it all. It's rarely an altruistic and optional choice to roll out of bed, jump in the shower, dress for success, commute to work, eat lunch at our desk, sit through another meeting, and leave our unfinished to-do list on our desk before heading out for the commute back home.

We work because we have to.

We work because we have bills to pay and mouths to feed.

We work to pay off the student loans we thought would lead to bigger paychecks.

We work to earn the money we need to pay for the lives we have, and to create the ones we want.

Over the past 20+ years spending time in corporate classrooms across the country as a coach and facilitator, I've worked with plenty of kick-ass women, who are doing kick-ass work, and who are highly engaged in what they do. However, those same kick-ass women talk about the inner ass kicking that comes from the sacrifices they are making to their own health and well-being in the pursuit of professional success and growth. They lament over their inability to find "work-life balance" (WTF is that anyway?), and the constant pull of conflicting priorities. As often as not they talk about feeling exhausted rather than empowered, resigned rather than renewed, and overwhelmed more than overjoyed. They bring up anxiety over an uncertain future rather than anticipation of good things to come, and they are filled with as much inner confusion as inner peace. And those are the women who claim to like their work! Those who don't, who are there because they feel trapped, who feel that they are without another option and can't make a different choice or step out in a new direction? They echo all of that same inner turmoil, but within the context of working at a job where they are just tying to make ends meet by making it through the day. Day after day after day. Ready for another glass of wine yet?

A lot of us are, and say so. I can't count the number of times I've overheard women in the workplace talking about their wine. They look forward to it, can't wait for it, can already taste it, made sure to put it in the fridge so it will be chilled when they get home, are stopping on the way from work to buy it, are meeting friends after work for a half-price glass or two, or are picking up a bottle to take back to their hotel room. For some, it is even an end-of-the-day ritual with a few colleagues

BEFORE leaving the office.

Recently, a friend of mine, a counselor for a small rural school, told me that she had experienced a particularly rough week at work. A 42-year-old married mother of three, she loves her students, has known many of them since their first day of school, and feels it deeply when they share deeply painful things with her. After an especially draining day where she felt like she couldn't absorb one more drop of pain, all she could think about was getting home and draining an entire bottle of wine. She resisted the urge with a brilliant strategy. She burst into the kitchen, burst into tears, and then told her husband in no uncertain terms to stand between her and her wine bottle. And then she sat down, had another good cry, told him about the day and let it all slowly drain away. Brilliant.

Feel it.

Say it.

Ask for help.

I love her story because I think it clearly illuminates a widely shared sentiment when it comes to women, our work, and our wine; we are worn out, worn thin and sometimes feel like we might not make it through another day. Pouring our nightly glass(es) of wine feels like it smooths out our ragged edges and eases us through the rest of another over-filled day, until we finally fall into bed, praying for the increasingly illusive good night of sleep. (Which, of course, is even more illusive because of the wine we drink.) And then we get up the next morning and do it all again.

Whether we live to work or work to live, we also work to get paid, and beyond our paycheck, compensation can come in many different currencies: Health benefits. Paid vacation. Funding a more secure retirement. Power. Satisfaction. The chance to make a contribution to something greater than ourselves. A sense of accomplishment. A means of growth and further learning. The chance to use our gifts and abilities. Finding appreciation, respect and acknowledgment for the efforts we make, the results we produce and the impacts we have. Social interaction. Creating a better life than the one we grew up with. To get out of the house and away from the kids. Only you know why you show up at work day after day, and whether or not it is working for you.

Our lives are best served when we are able to connect who we are with what we do and how we do it. When those dots don't connect, discontentment is inevitable, causing us to question almost everything about ourselves and our work. Am I investing too much in work at the expense of my own health? In succeeding at work am I failing at home? Will I ever earn the money I deserve? Is this the road to a promotion or a dead end street? Will I always have to work harder than my male colleagues to prove my value? Do I really have what it takes to get where I'm going? Am I doing the right thing? Will I ever get to do the work I really want? Hard questions with no easy answers.

Among the many things we may look for from our work, it seems fair to say that satisfaction and contentment should be high on our list. If you spend one-third (or more) of your waking hours at work, finding meaning and satisfaction in the work-wedge of your daily pie matters. Raise your hand if you've ever left work, looking forward to nothing more than that first sip of wine; to the relaxation that happens as the knots in your stomach begin to loosen their grip, the anxiety that begins to ease, the frustration that drops down a notch, the resentment that gets sent to bed early without supper, the fear of failure that momentarily fades away, and the stress that with each mouthful becomes a little less stressful. All when you pour that first glass of wine. Keep your hand up if you've also ever walked into the house after work, gone straight to the kitchen, and poured yourself a glass of wine before ever taking your off your coat or unloading the groceries (which, of course, include another bottle of wine just in case it's been "one of those days"). If your hand is still up in the air, I'm with you sister! Been there. Done that.

So why can the work we do drive us to drink too much of the wine we love? A few possible reasons come to mind. If you love your job but are underpaid, it's easy to overindulge in wine to compensate for the frustration. If you hate your job but love the big paycheck, wine can numb the inner compromise. When your work is good, but the only feedback you receive is how it could be better, nothing sounds better than a lovely glass of wine as a pat on your own tired back. If the glass ceiling seems shatterproof, a glass of wine is a shot in the arm. Unfortunately, drinking wine won't move our contentment needle in the right direction.

When Tom and I got married back in 1994 I was working as a human resources manager for a highly successful, upscale retail organization known for their world-class service. It was a great job. I was good at it, enjoyed it and received plenty of acknowledgment for work well done. But. Inside a small mutiny was starting to rumble. I was ready for a change. Our daughters were on the brink of adolescence, and I wanted to be more available to our growing-up girls than my current career path allowed. Summers, weekends and holidays were the worst. While those were the times for family fun, family celebrations and family vacations, those were also the times when sales were the strongest and hours the longest. It started to feel like I was selling my soul to the company store. A great company store to be sure, but selling my soul nonetheless. For a while my nightly glasses of wine kept me and my inner misery company.

About that time, my artist BFF Kristine invited me to join her in the practice of something called "morning pages," a simple exercise from Julia Cameron's classic book, *The Artist's Way*[33]. Get out of bed and write three pages of long hand, stream of consciousness thoughts. No inner editing allowed. That's it. Three pages. Every day. And every day, regardless of what else showed up on those three pages, the words "I want to quit my job" appeared. First as a whisper, then a polite request, until finally all three pages were filled with the same line: "I FUCKING WANT TO QUIT MY JOB!"

Ok already. I hear you. Having just purchased a big home to let our newly formed clan spread out, my income was essential, so I needed a little more information before jumping ship. Each morning I asked my inner self, "If you want to quit this job, what do you want to do instead?" As it turned out, my inner self knew, as she usually does if I give her the chance to speak up. Day by day, I wrote my way to the answer. I wanted to write a book, speak, and try my hand at corporate training and coaching. Had I done any of that before? No. But apparently I wanted to try.

If there was ever any doubt that I married a great guy, his response to my desire to quit erased it for good. Here is loosely what that conversation looked like:

Me: I want to quit my job.

Him: (Deep breath) When?

Me: Now.

Him: (Deeper breath) And do what?

Me: I'm not sure, but I think it includes writing a book, public speaking and corporate training and coaching.

Him: (Long pause) Any opportunities on the horizon?

Me: None that I can see.

Him: (Long pause AND deep breath) Mol, if that is what your heart is telling you to do, then you should do it. We'll figure it out.

And so I did it. And we figured it out.

It was unlike anything I had done before, and it ended up better than I could have imagined. But it took trusting my inner leading enough to leave the safe harbor of a secure job with only growth and advancement ahead, and sail out into uncharted waters. Andre Gide said, "One does not discover new lands without consenting to lose sight of the shore for a very long time."[34] Thankfully for me, it wasn't a long time, nor could we afford for it to be.

As it turned out, Kristine's morning pages told her she wanted to write a book too, and within a matter of months we stumbled upon an idea for a book. Within a shorter matter of months we signed a contract with a publisher for *Letters to Our Daughters*[35], which, when published, was highlighted on The Oprah Show, led to a cross-country book tour, and continuing speaking opportunities[36]. During those same early months I connected with and formed a long relationship with a training and consulting firm right in my back yard. Thankfully, I was fortunate enough to have the option to leave one thing before knowing what the next one was. That hasn't always been the case, but this time it was. Yes, I needed to find new work quickly. Just not the very next day.

If work is sucking the life out of us, sipping more wine won't help. If the job is too all consuming, consuming more wine isn't the answer. If a career move is called for, wine won't move us further down that trail. Reality may dictate that you stay put while you seek a better option. If so, then by all means, stay put, and, use any means necessary to begin the trail to a better place. From my experience, wine won't help us get anywhere good sooner, faster or better.

Perhaps the question for those of us who love our wine a bit too much is: To pour or not to pour? If nightly wine is our exit strategy, a way of escaping the hard work of looking more closely at our work, another glass only delays our eventual reckoning. We need a different strategy, a way of shifting our situation, our mindset, or both. A shift is necessary because our work matters. It is part of who we are and a piece of our contribution, large or small, to the planet we all share. We need to either find our way to work that matters to us, or work in a way that matters regardless of what we do.

9

KILLING ME SOFTLY
WITH HIS SONG

*Why do we drink wine when we're
thirsty for love?*

∽

"It's strange what the mind can do when the heart is
giving the directions."[37]

NICOLE KRAUSS

LOVE IS KIND OF LIKE A HOME for your heart. Like any house, it is best built with a good design, on a strong foundation, using quality materials. Formal vows or not, long term commitment or short-term romance, arranged marriage or one of our own choosing, young or old, male, female or somewhere in between, we're looking for love. Underneath it all, I believe we want a partner to love who will love us back, be an equal-half rather than a better one, will show up and do what it takes, and be in it for the long haul. As I understand love, it is meant to provide safe lodging. It is a port in our storm, a harbor-of-grace, a warm hearth, a place to lay our weary heads, and a table laid with food for our souls.

On the other not-so-safe hand, love is high-risk adventure. High risk because there are no guarantees. Sometimes despite all of our efforts, our deep desires to make it work, and our hopes which spring eternal, love just doesn't work out. The person we love dies, goes astray, falls out of love with us or simply can't or won't do what it takes to keep going. And, vice versa. But I'll stake my life on the belief that it is an adventure worth risking. Love can take us places we would never go on our own, show us the hidden wonders of our internal worlds, lead us to new heights and secret underground caves. It is the place where we can be known and loved as we are, dressed only in our naked truth. Love is the deal. Love is the thing. Love is what we want. Love is what we need. It's simple. Love makes the world go round. It is not however, easy. No way. No how. Love is hard work. Love is painful. Love is exhausting. Love is complicated, and it <u>does</u> mean having to say you are sorry. Usually, a lot. Love is costly. To put it mildly, love is not for the faint of heart. But. Nothing compares to it. Love is worth the effort. Love has the power to heal. Love is exhilarating, and at its best it is a two-way street paved with grace and forgiveness. Love is priceless. It is however, completely different than falling in love. That's the easy part. Knowing who to fall in love with? That, my friends, is the tricky part. Like Tevye's daughters in *Fiddler on the Roof*[38], we are looking for a match of our own, and will go to great lengths to find it.

We've come a long way from Yenta, the village matchmaker, having left the village and logged onto the World Wide Web. Want to find love? There's an app for that. According to Wikipedia, "Tinder is a location-based dating and social discovery application (using Facebook) that facilitates communication between mutually interested users, allowing matched users to chat."[39] Mutually interested users? Just makes your heart go pitter-pat, doesn't it. No? Well, to each her own. A right swipe can lead to the right match. Are you more of a clicker than a swiper? A quick search will serve up a smorgasbord of sites and services to suit almost any taste. From Match.com[40] to Farmersonly.com[41], Amish-Online-Dating[42] to Gluten Free Singles[43], there is a dating site for you. However, all the technology in the world, all the speed dating, matchmaking, networking and putting ourselves "out there" won't guarantee finding the love we seek. Like I said, it's tricky. In order to find true love, one needs to be true to oneself. Pretty hard if one hasn't figured one's self out yet. It's so much more fun to get swept away in love's current, then to paddle upstream into our own lives and fall in love with the woman we find there.

As the saying goes, any port in the storm will do. But it shouldn't. For more years than I like to admit, my own criteria when looking for love couldn't have been more straightforward. You like me? Find me attractive? Want to go out with me? Sold! I usually went to the lowest bidder, my dating track record speaking for itself. Boyfriend number one was later arrested as an armed and dangerous stalker. After the future felon came the alcoholic cowboy, followed by the married alcoholic cowboy. It went downhill from there. When I was twenty-two, my future ex-husband proposed to me, in a bar, after dating for a week. The answer was obvious, because as the song says, love is all you need. I'd found someone to love me, and somehow that seemed like enough. Thirsty for love, I never stopped to consider that there might be more to the story.

Planning a big church wedding, there was more than enough to distract me from actually thinking about what I was doing. Preoccupied with choosing a wedding dress, color scheme and flowers, it was easy to ignore the smoldering anger beneath a handsome and charming surface, differing values around almost everything, and world views that didn't jive. People have asked me when I knew I'd made the wrong choice. Sadly, for both of us, I knew before I walked down the aisle. As apparently almost thirty percent of us girls do.[44] But what's a girl to do? What if this was my only shot at love? My best offer?

The only offer?

A few weeks before the wedding my mom did the most courageous thing. She found me behind closed doors crying, again, over another angry downpour that had rained on my already soggy wedding parade. "Honey," she quietly said, "are you sure about this? We can call the whole thing off." Desperately looking for the courage to take her up on that offer, all I could find was the fear of letting everyone, including myself, down. Call off the grand wedding we had planned? Waste thousands of my parents' hard-earned dollars? Face the questions from those who only saw what looked from the outside like a dazzling match? Find myself single, alone and adrift in a world I hadn't yet learned to navigate on my own? Tuning out my inner song, which had been desperately trying to get my attention from the beginning, the only music I could hear were strains of "Here Comes the Bride.[45]"

Our song is always ready to lead us out of harm's way and home to ourselves, if we have the courage to listen. But at that point in my life, I didn't. And so, up the aisle I marched, misgivings, fears and all and said, "I do." Yes, I do promise to tolerate bad moods and temper tantrums, road rage and kicked doors. Yes, I do agree to live with the fear of hands that throw objects and fists that punch holes in walls. And yes, I do choose to settle and survive rather than set out on my own and thrive.

I hitched my wagon to his for the next 13 years, and wine was part of my survival strategy. I guess you could say that wine was part of what kept me from falling off the marriage wagon. As each day drew to a close, and dinner simmered on the stove, I would light the candles and pour the wine. That familiar evening ritual, now a longtime habit, helped me to pretend for that" happy hour", that our home was too. But for me, it wasn't. It wasn't a safe harbor or a port in the storm, because the storm that was always brewing was looming under my own roof. As wine softened the emotional blows of the day, I would convince myself, again, that I could make it work. Uncertain as I was when I made those vows at the front of the church, once made I meant to keep them. Especially now, with two little girl in the picture. I felt stuck between a rock and a hard place. And we all know stuck. The feeling that we won't ever get out of our situation, job, money woes, family dramas, illness, and of course, relationships. Stuck totally sucks. Downing a little wine helps us forget we are stuck. Until the next morning. Wine can help us put off the hard decision until tomorrow. Or next week. Or next month. Or next…. when it will still be there waiting for us. At some point, if we want it to be different, we have to do something different.

So why do we get stuck in the first place? Why do we allow ourselves to enter into relationships that don't serve us? That ask us to compromise who we are and what we stand for? That take more than they give? That look right on the outside, but feel wrong on the inside? That feel safe on the surface, but put us in danger at the core? Relationships that we would never let our best friend settle for? Relationships that may be with a perfectly fine person, but simply aren't a good fit? If love is priceless, why are we willing to settle for a cheap imitation?

Why. Do. We. Do. It???

For days I've been trying to figure out the answer as I struggle to write this chapter. I wanted my answer to be clever and witty, complex and wise. It wasn't working, as I kept deleting twice as much as I kept. Finally, sitting at my desk, wondering if it was too early for a wee glass of wine, I remembered one of the essential rules for writing; writers need to walk, or in this case, snowshoe. So I got my frustrated ass up out of the chair, strapped on my snowshoes and headed back down our road. At about the same spot in the road as that first evening walk, it hit me. I had been making it way too complicated. It just plain ain't that difficult. We do it, because we are afraid. Period. End of story. Afraid that this is as good as it gets, and we may never get another chance, much less a better one. We're afraid of the unknown, and at least this relationship is familiar. We're afraid of being alone, having never learned to be our own best company. Afraid of hurting their feelings, we stuff our own. Fear of losing the good opinion of others, we ignore our own best judgment. It's scary to think about making it on our own, if, having married for love, we're now staying for the money. Perhaps at the deepest level, we're afraid that we aren't enough. We aren't good enough, attractive enough, successful enough, strong enough, intelligent enough, young enough, old enough, or maybe even anything enough, so better make a go of this one. Wine is a way to distance ourselves from the heart-stopping fear of not being enough, of not being worthy of more. It lulls us into thinking that things aren't so bad. It could be worse. It might get better. He/she is doing the best they can. And well, they love me. When it comes to the places in our hearts, like Sally Field in her Oscar acceptance speech, we find ourselves saying, "I can't deny the fact that you like me... right now... you like me."[46] And, as we pour ourselves another glass of wine, we convince ourselves that is enough. But it isn't.

The need for love is fundamental. After water, food and shelter, we are hardwired to find love and drag it back to our cave. But Cupid's arrow can easily miss the mark, because choosing a good partner when we haven't first learned to walk in partnership with our own soul, is a major crapshoot. Love has to begin as an inside job, and venture out from there. It starts with intimately coming to know ourselves, who we are and what we care about. What we want out of life and where we want it to take us. What we value in others, and the type of person with whom we want to share our hearts. Without that first-hand knowledge it's easy to settle for second-rate love.

One of the primary keys to love and intimacy, according to clinical psychologist and world-renown sex and marital therapist, Dr. David Schnarsch, is found in something called "differentiation." Dr. Schnarsch, co-director of the Marriage and Family Health Center in Evergreen, Colorado, and author of the book *Passionate Marriage*[47], explains differentiation as "the dynamic process through which you can live in close proximity to a partner and still maintain a separate sense of self." He goes on to say, "the best marital brew is neither dependence nor independence, but a balanced state of interdependence."[48] Looking elsewhere for acceptance and love when we haven't first found it within ourselves will always leave us thirsting for more. And wine, I'm sorry to say, will never quench a love-thirsty soul. Trust me on that one.

Maybe I needed to stay in my first marriage that long in order to find my way back to myself. I don't know. I do know that wine made it easier to stay. Nightly glasses of wine slurred the words of my inner voice that wanted to be heard. Seeking solace in my lovely wine glass kept me from facing not only the disappointment in a failing marriage, but also in myself for settling for a mismatch in the first place. It numbed the pain enough that I didn't have to look at the rock (destructive marriage) or the hard place (the seemingly impossible road out) between which I felt caught. Getting stuck where we don't want to be, is one way to figure out where we do.

After thirteen years, I felt more stuck than ever. And then something shifted. In the midst of another heated argument with him, I saw our daughters watching us from the doorway. They were afraid. At that moment, my inner voice, the one I had been squelching ever since not teaching that class all those years ago in college, threw her hand up in the air, and demanded to be heard. "You've done all you can," she sang. "It's time to go." This time I found the courage to listen. In that instant, I made the decision to leave, and suddenly I wasn't stuck. Taking action on our own behalf is the key to unlocking any door behind which we're trapped.

For years I'd heard that God hates divorce. Like the children's nursery rhyme, the bible told me so. I get it. Divorce rips lives apart, can damage relationships for years to come, hurts children as much or more than the adults who can't make it work, and costs more than any amount ever shelled out to the lawyers. Circling through the debris of divorce can be a lifelong process, with a lingering sadness over losing one's family, and anyone who has ever lived through a divorce hopes never to do so again. Not to put myself on equal footing with the Almighty, but I hate divorce too, and believe there is something we both hate even more: when we stay in relationships that do more harm than good.

When I finally found the courage to leave, my biggest fear was that God would stay behind at church, leaving me to fend for myself. My greatest surprise was finding that God came with me, helped me pack my bags, carry them from my old life and load them into the new, quietly humming my melody until I could remember it again. Over time, the tears of sadness over my divorce and the years I could never get back, turned into ones of gratitude for a new chance at life and love. It felt like a miracle. Kind of like when Jesus turned water into wine at a wedding.

10

THE SOUND OF SILENCE

How do we lose our voice?

⤶

"It took me quite a long time to develop a voice, and
now that I have it, I'm not going to be silent."[49]
MADELEINE ALBRIGHT

TO SING REQUIRES A VOICE. In the biblical story of
creation, God's voice speaks the world into being. "Let
there be light. And there was light."[50] With the power
of Her voice the world was created. Every day more of
the world came into being as He raised His voice in the
song of creation. Looking out over the holy ground of
Her masterpiece, She saw that it was good, and said so.
I like to imagine it went something like, "Damn Girl!
You're good!" That's what I would have said if I had just
created the heavens and the earth.

Like the Great Creator, the power of our voice is
immense. We are each tiny little creators, speaking our

own lives into being. With it we come out of closets or lock ourselves in someone else's skin, take leaps of faith or cling to the guardrail, tie a knot in the end of our rope or dig our pits a little deeper, ask for a well-deserved raise or settle for what we are offered, create loving relationships or stay in toxic ones, accuse the rapist in spite of our fear or suffer in shame because of it, ask for help or flounder and fall, ask for forgiveness or defend our transgressions. Our voice resonates through every thought, word, choice and action. And since actions speak louder than words, sometimes we speak the loudest without uttering a word. Rosa Parks didn't stand up and give a speech. She sat down and changed the world.

If, as this book supposes, we are here to sing our song, then a voice is what we need. If that's what we need, what, exactly then, is it? To begin with, it is the utterance of sound produced by the larynx, often referred to - interestingly enough - as the voice box. My friend David Berry, who writes and speaks about the voice of leadership in his book, *A More Daring Life: Finding Voice At The Crossroads of Change*, wanted to know the source of the voice, and so started with basic geography. Where was it? Curious, he measured it. Went to his drawer, got out a ruler, and found that on him, exactly 18 inches between his cerebral cortex behind his forehead, and his heart, in the middle of his chest, sits his voice box.[51] David believes, and rightly so, that in order to lead and live well, both head and heart must be engaged, and it is the voice that connects the two. His insightful exercise goes straight to the heart of the matter, since it is our voice that connects the dots between our cerebral gray matter and our blood-red hearts. It is our voice that expresses not only what we know, but also what we believe. It conveys both what we think, and how we feel. Whether through verbal communication, the written word, sign-language, casting our votes on ballots and with bank accounts, or refusing to move to the back of the bus, our voice is the instrument through which we express who we are to the world.

In the beginning, using our voice comes naturally. The newborn's cry announces her arrival into the world. Wrapped up in a blanket all warm and tight, she gets her first singing lesson in the might of her own voice. "I'm hungry and somebody better do something about it!" she wails. Expecting to be heard, she usually is. Somewhere along the way though, all of that changes. The further we go, the harder it gets to hang on to our voice, as life, our parents, the school bully, teachers, our manager, the rabid radio talk-show host, our pastor or rabbi, family, peers or well-meaning friends attempt to teach us that speaking up isn't safe. They suggest that ours is the wrong tune, and that we are singing in the wrong key. As it turns our, according to them, our feelings, thoughts, ideas and perspectives aren't the right ones. Our choices and actions march to the beat of the wrong drum. Our opinions, beliefs and questions make others uncomfortable. They politely ask us to pipe down. More to the point, they would be much happier if we would just shut the fuck up already.

Historically, as in what feels like forever, women have had to fight to have a voice. It was a painfully slow march to the right to be heard, as women fought for the right to vote. We marched and demonstrated, picketed and refused to eat, were arrested, bullied and beaten, all in the pursuit of having a voice, of having a say in the state of our union. While we may have made progress, it is still a work in progress. From the classroom to the living room, the boardroom to the bedroom, and everywhere in between, having a say in the state of our own personal union can still feel like an uphill battle. How many of us have finally mustered the courage to speak up, say what we really mean, express our excitement over what we want to do, accomplish, attempt, have, become? Or spoken up on our own behalf, stating what we want or need, or asked the question that no one else is brave enough to raise? Only to be dismissed, overruled, ignored, ridiculed or criticized. Do that one too many times and it becomes easier to just keep it to ourselves, put a lid on it, tone it down, go with the flow even if it kills you. Which, by the way, it will. Maybe not right away, but eventually the sound of our silence strangles our voice.

In losing our voice, we lose our song, which can only lead to sorrow. Sorrow is that deepest kind of distress born of disappointment and loss, and one would be hard pressed to find a woman who hasn't experienced that kind of sadness at some point in her life. Times when she didn't speak up, take a stand, or make a different choice. Times when she chose to remain silent because speaking up was just too hard. Or scary. Or exhausting. And yet, it feels like a deep and universal truth that finding our voice is one of our most important tasks. Using it, one of our most awesome responsibilities. Raising it truthfully, one of our highest callings. The act of creation continues, out in the world and inside our own lives, and it continues through the instrument of our voice.

Knowing we have a voice is one thing. Learning how to use it quite another, and at some point, most of us need voice lessons. The good news? There are voice teachers all around. The not-so-good news? The ones that can teach us the most are usually the ones we welcome the least! Like, for example, my ex-husband.

The voice that had gotten me into that marriage needed to learn a new language to get me out. In leaving him, I had reclaimed my voice. Ending the marriage however, was only the beginning of learning how to use it again. Lucky for me, every day was a new opportunity to practice, as I struggled to negotiate a divorce settlement that I could live with, including child support, custody terms and visitation rights. It required me to connect my head and my heart through the instrument of my voice. And it was hard. There were times when I thought I couldn't do it, even as I knew that I had to. It was like a voice lesson crash course. On crack. I'm not sure I've ever been more frightened. Spiders or putting on a bikini didn't even come close. Most of our conversations were held over the phone, and on those calls I usually talked…Way. Too. Much. I justified, explained, reasoned, pleaded, cried and yelled until I was hoarse. Every call left me exhausted and defeated, feeling weak and ashamed at my inability to stand my ground, hold onto myself and speak the truth. There were more than a few nights that more than a few glasses of wine soothed my battle wounds. But the next day, the war still raged.

In the movie, *The King's Speech*[52], King George VI hired a voice teacher to help him overcome his stutter and find his voice, so that he could lead his people through World War II. Like him, I needed help to overcome my fear and find my voice for the warfare on my own home front. That help was found through my most trusted friend and some index cards.

After another draining phone call, sitting with Kristine and probably over a bottle of wine, we decided that I needed a tool. Something that would help me say what

I meant and mean what I said. Period. Thus, was born the 3x5 card. It was a simple tool for a difficult task. First, determine my message for the next encounter, choosing new vows, different from the ones made in front of the church years earlier. Yes, I do expect regular, timely child support payments. No, I'm not willing to skip a month because things are tight for you. Yes, I am asking the court for full custody. And No, I'm not kidding.

Those 3x5 cards became my mantra, my lyrics, and my lifeline. I wrote out a card for each issue to be resolved and question to be answered. They were short, not sweet, and to the point, and I was never without them. They were tucked into my handbag or pocket, sitting on my nightstand, taped to the mirror, and in my desk drawer. The next time the phone rang, I answered, put the call on hold to buy a little time (always a good move), grabbed those 3x5 cards, took a deep breath, and held a new kind of conversation. Fewer words, more meaning. When tempted to take the bait, those cards kept me off the hook. Feeling the urge to jump back in, they kept me on my dock. I learned to be still, and let my words hang in the air, the silence allowing me to breathe rather than waste my breath. Shaking like a leaf as I hung up the phone after that first index-card-led conversation, I realized that I hadn't felt that brave in years. Scared and courageous all in the same breath, which is usually how it goes. Like the Duke said, "Courage is being scared to death and saddling up anyway." More calls, more cards, until one day I found that I didn't need a cue card. I'd found my voice.

It's always there for us. Our voice has our back, and will back us up every time if we let it. No matter who or what has shut us up in the past, an eternal choice exists in the present moment to find it, warm it up and raise it again. The more we use it, the less chance of losing it. But, what do we do when it does goes missing? (Spoiler alert: It will.) How do we find it again? (We can.)

A couple of years ago my iPad was stolen. On vacation in Florida for a wedding, staying in a lovely rental cottage, we returned from a morning outing to find that someone had broken in and taken it. A couple of hours later I was speaking with the police woman who came to take a report of the robbery, giving her as many details as I could about the missing iPad: color of the case, version, any identifying marks, etc. Did I have the "Find my iPad" app she wanted to know? Yes, as a matter of fact, I did. Was it activated? No, as a matter of fact, it wasn't.

While the iPad was never recovered, that experience made me think about finding our voice if it gets lost or stolen. As it turns out, our internal hard drive comes loaded with our very own loss-prevention application, designed to protect our inner voice from loss and theft.

Like any application, it has to be activated in order to work, so here are a few steps to get you started:

1. Go to Settings. (Core beliefs: At the deepest level, what matters to me?)
2. Tap Find MyVoice. (In this case, what do you think, feel, know, or believe? What needs to be said?)
3. Sign in with your user name. (Your most authentic self. The true-blue you.)
4. Turn on Find My Voice. (Get quiet, tune in, trust what you hear, and follow your own lead.)

You'll know it when you hear it.

You will.

If you're not sure, ask for help, because sometimes it takes a village to raise a voice, which means staying in relationship with those who recognize your voice, and can alert you when they hear a stranger's words coming out of your mouth. Whenever you say or do something contrary to who you are, what you care about and what you believe, a bit of your voice gets lost. Those are the times you need the people who love you enough to tenderly wrap their arms around you, and bring you back to yourself, by gently saying, "Where is my friend/sister/mother/daughter/colleague/partner/teammate, and what the fuck have you done with her?"

It takes courage to say what we mean, knowing that doing so might result in conflict, rejection, judgment, criticism, or all of the above. Taking a stand for what we believe can land us squarely in the hot seat with those we care about the most. Speaking up can cost us our job. Telling it like it is can end a relationship. Advocating for ourselves can leave us out in the cold. Looking back I can see that one of the ways I coped with the frustration when I felt unheard, the resentment from taking a backseat too many times, and the pain from being ignored, was by having one more glass of wine until it didn't hurt quite so much. Under the influence, we can convince ourselves that speaking up won't matter anyway. Nothing we might say will right that wrong, save that relationship, or change the outcome. Our words will surely fall on deaf ears. But in the middle of the night, when no one else can hear our thoughts, and we're awake, because that is what too much wine will do to a girl, we are sad and disappointed that we didn't find the courage to speak up.

What are the gutsy conversations waiting for your voice? What changes and choices are listening for your call to action? What chances, risks, and challenges are awaiting your marching orders?

Instead of wine, how about some 3x5 cards?

11

A MAZE OF GRACE

*How does wine cause forgotten memories
and remembered regrets?*

⌒

"The business of life is the acquisition of memories.
In the end, that's all there is."

MR. CARSON - DOWNTON ABBEY

EXTENDING GRACE IN ANY DIRECTION can be difficult.
Offering it to ourselves, perhaps the furthest reach of
all. When it comes to this wine thing, for me, grace has
been required. Because of too much wine there have
been moments that I can't remember and regrets that I
wish I could forget. Life happens a moment at a time.
Always has. Always will. All of our moments are strung
together, and that stringing together is our life. Some
moments are better than others. Sometimes we get it
right. Other times, so wrong we're not sure if we will
ever recover. If that doesn't call for amazing grace, I

don't know what does.

When my youngest daughter graduated from college, it was a cause for joy and celebration if there ever was one. Like all of us at one time or another, she had fought a mighty battle. Hers was different than yours, mine or anyone else's as all struggles are, and yet, in the personal is found the universal. Suffice it to say, we were all gathered together to celebrate and cheer as she marched across that stage in her cap and gown. Tall, strong, smart, beautiful, rebellious and confident. That's my girl.

Our tribe showed up in force for the graduation in Montana. Some drove, others flew, and airline miles were shared. People did what it took to be there. We stayed in two fabulous cabins on the banks of a wild river on the outskirts of town. It was magical. The weather was perfect. Every day started as the sun came up over the river and we gathered, one by one, around the outdoor fire with blankets and coffee. Each evening ended under the stars around that same fire. Think *A River Runs Through It*[53] meets Ralph Lauren.

We have a kind of tradition, a ritual in our family. When honoring one of our own, we gather around the table or in front of the fire, and pay tribute to the guest of honor. We share what we see in them, their gifts and strengths. We tell stories that border on a roast, but end in a heartfelt toast. We love on them. And love on them. And then we love on them some more. The night of graduation, after dinner we settled together around the fire. As people shared their stories and memories I watched her face as she hung on every word, her soul filled to overflowing. At the end of every toast, she got up and made her way in the firelight to whomever was speaking and loved back on them with a hug, a kiss, some tears. It was her moment. In fact, it was a couple of hours of sacred moments that she will remember forever. I, on the other hand, won't. It wasn't that I drank my way through two bottles of wine. But I had a glass or two too many so that I don't remember with clarity all that was said.

I can't ever get those moments back.

Ever.

When it was my turn, I had a gift for her. A simple, engraved sterling silver dog tag on a long, delicate chain. Classic, tender, strong, just like her. She opened it up, tears falling as she listened. I do remember most of what I said. I told a story of the fierce independence and determination that were hers from the beginning. When she was learning to drive we insisted that she, like her sisters, learn to drive a clutch. Our sessions always ended in tears. Usually mine. Teaching your own child to drive is sort of like jamming a sliver in your own finger. Why would you ever do that? Finally, in typical fashion, she took the car keys, got in the '78 Volvo, and for three hours drove around, and around, and around our cul-d-sac. And then she drove around again. The gears ground. And ground. And ground. Until finally they didn't. She had mastered the art of the clutch. On her own. In her own way. In her own time. Once she sets her mind to something, that something gets done. Like her graduation.

As I ended my toast, she got up and came over to me with her necklace. She asked me to put it on. As I stood up, I was a tad unsteady, my brain a little foggy. Rather than dropping it around her neck and closing the clasp in that "this is special" tender, just-so sort of way, I left it closed and pulled it on over her head. Even as she continued to ask me if I would please put it around her neck. Please? Instead, I struggled it over her head. It was beautiful. She loved it. And the next day, it broke my heart.

The moment was gone.

No do-overs.

I talked to Lauren about the graduation necklace when I first started writing this book. Her grace was amazing. Mine, on the other hand, is still a bit jagged around the edges. It's a memory that returns to haunt me, and perhaps…that's not such a bad thing. I wonder how many other moments are lost in the fog of one more glass. Like movie endings that I've missed, curled up on the couch with my daughters for a girl's-night, because my eyes were too heavy? Or an important conversation with a loved one that needed to wait until everyone else was in bed? What regrets have I created under wine's influence? Like the time I told the brother of a friend to "get the fuck out of the kitchen" when he offered to help with the Thanksgiving dishes. Now there's some classy gratitude for you.

As I travel back to those times, I search for the grace to accept those experiences as teachers. Gifts of hindsight that cast a light on the possibility of doing it differently in the future. Now I find myself thinking about an upcoming event or celebration, an evening with family and friends, or simply the end of another day, and ask myself how I want to feel at the end of the time. The answer to that question has become simply, "I want to be present." Knowing that being present is my desired destination, I am able to more mindfully choose how to get there. I guess the old adage about sums it up: Begin with the end in mind.

This past year my son-in-law graduated from the same university. We traveled over rivers and through woods back to Montana to celebrate his accomplishments. His gift? A silver engraved dog tag to match hers. He didn't ask me to put it on for him. That's a girl thing. However, the memory of that night is clear. As he opened his gift, read his card, made his way to give me a hug, I caught my daughter's eye across the room. We shared an understanding and recognition of the grace surrounding that moment.

The memory from that earlier night on the river around that fire brings back the words from the Episcopal liturgy that I still remember from early years at church. "We've done those things that we ought not to have done. And left undone those things that we ought to have done"[54] I ought not to have had those extra glasses of wine. I ought to have slipped that necklace around her neck. Forgotten memories and remembered regrets are tenacious traveling companions. Only grace can loosen their grip. Trust me. I know.

12

TRY A LITTLE TENDERNESS

Why is caring well for ourselves so damn hard?

∽

"We need to do a better job of putting ourselves
higher on our own 'to do' list."[55]

MICHELLE OBAMA

IN HER SONG, *I Am Woman*,[56] Helen Reddy reminded us that as women…well…we roar. And indeed we can, we do, we should. The world is in desperate need of our voice. However, we also do something else. The first line of that song could go something like this: "I am woman, watch me serve." Women are affirmed for the love and care we extend outward, acknowledged and given more responsibility for commitment and long hours at work, and appreciated for our efforts made on behalf of others. A gold star doesn't often appear on our charts however, when we take time to care for ourselves. Recently, I told someone that I was getting a massage later that day. Her response? "Well aren't you the pampered one." Implied in her comment is that anything a woman does for herself is a luxury. An option. A negotiable. Something to be considered once the needs of others have been met. Something to squeeze into a rare gap in her schedule. To be honest, I've enviously thought the same thing myself when seeing another woman spend time and money on her own self-care.

Most of us don't need an external response from someone else to feel bad about doing something good for ourselves. We're perfectly capable of undermining our own attempts at self-care with self-imposed guilt for being so, well, selfish. How can we go to the gym for a workout when it means scheduling a meeting at a time that isn't "convenient" for the other person? What kind of daughter are we if we don't answer the next phone call from our aging mom or dad, knowing that hearing our voice is the only highlight in another lonely day? How dare we say no to another project at work when everyone else is already stretched so thin? And if we do for the sake of our sanity, our health, our family or all of the above, will we be passed over for that promised promotion? How can we opt out of hosting Thanksgiving dinner, when the rest of the family is counting on us? Won't it cause financial hardship for our kids if we don't take care of our grandchildren? Every time we are asked?

It feels like a win-lose proposition. Take care of ourselves and neglect the needs of others. Trust our own voice and ignore his, hers, theirs. Do what we know is right for us but feels wrong to someone that we care about. When we're bitchy because we are in need of care, extending it to ourselves makes us feel like selfish bitches. What right do any of us girls have to think about me, myself and I, when there is him, her and them in need? It's a catch-22. Care for ourselves and fill up with guilt. Care for others and choke on resentment. Like a sedative, wine can dull either one for the night, and quite honestly, that is why I think so many of us love our wine. We have come to count on it at the end of another long day spent tending to the needs of others above our own. That first sip feels like self-care. Another glass gives us the sense that we are being good to ourselves, even if we are slurping it down while schlepping the shit someone else should have picked up and put away. It's just what we do. But endless service is a dangerous hill to pick, with a slippery slope to martyrdom waiting for us at the bottom. If not careful, our sacrifices to care for others become a badge of honor, our exhaustion a symbol of our selflessness. Finding room for one more morsel on our already heaping plates to feed the needs of others is the icing on our self-worth cake.

Underneath the urge to care for others before ourselves seems to lie a fundamental question: Do we even see ourselves as deserving of love and self-care? Or, are we trying to earn the right to finally feel worthy? It is a question worth considering, and Jesus (who incidentally was an early advocate for women) provides a clue when he says, "Love your neighbor (child, friend, partner, spouse, co-worker, store clerk, postal worker, in-laws, fill-in-the-blank) as yourself."[57] Hearing only the first part and eager to please and feel worthy, off we run to love and serve others at every opportunity. But it is a race to a nonexistent finish line since the needs are endless. Ignoring the second part, eventually we have nothing left to give, as our attempts to be selfless leave us less and less self from which to give.

If I love my neighbor as I often love myself, they will slam the door in my face the next time I knock! Jesus didn't say love yourself and screw your neighbor. It wasn't love yourself and to hell with everyone else. Not save yourself and let the poor suckers drown. Another great spiritual teacher, Lucille Ball, said it this way, "Love yourself first, and everything else falls in line. You really have to love yourself to get anything done in this world."[58] No wonder we loved Lucy.

The meaning behind both sage messages is that you are deserving of the same love and care that you extend to others. It is an unalienable right with which all are endowed. Making self-love, which includes self-care, a priority means we will have more of ourselves to give, and bring a stronger, more resilient and less resentful self to life's party. Seen in that light, self-care is an act of love and generosity. To ourselves, and everything and everyone around us, starting with those we care about the most. Although, at first none of us may see it that way. We will be changing a dance in which everyone involved knows the steps, and any attempt to change it means we will probably step on some toes. Be forewarned, as we begin to learn a new dance it will be awkward. We might feel selfish and guilty, while those who have come to count on us feel hurt and disregarded. Just keep dancing.

I can remember a time when choosing to meet my own needs first was really hard. Tom and I were attending a couple's weekend at a remote and rustic retreat center. It was designed to help us discover more about ourselves, as individuals and as partners. During an especially intense day, we learned that my primary needs include words of affirmation and lots of space and autonomy, while he requires physical touch and quality time together. I want him to tell me that I'm beautiful, and then disappear. He wants me to carve out time for him and reach out and touch… his hand, his neck, his arm, and of course, in the words of the one-man Broadway comedy, *Defending The Caveman*[59], to please, just "touch the weenie."

Late that evening we arrived back at our snow-covered cabin, exhausted, spent, and both in need of care.

All I wanted was for him to tell me he loved me, and move as far away as our 10x10 room would permit. He was ready to talk and touch. A lot. And not particularly in that order. It felt like an impossible proposition. Either-or. Win-lose. His needs or mine with no bridge between the two in sight. Asking for what I wanted led to guilt. Ignoring it, a highway paved with resentment. The safe and familiar thing to do would have been to focus on his needs, stuffing my own back into my basement where they belonged. I decided to try a different and daring approach. Tell him what I needed, which was to crawl into bed. My own to be specific, and pull the covers over my head.

And then morning came.

With a night of rest, I was ready for a good conversation and some quality time touching whatever wanted touching. With relish.

It felt selfish.

I was scared.

I did it anyway.

It worked.

And I'm still working on it.

Putting others out. Asking for help. Thinking about our own needs. None of these come naturally to most of us. With practice, they can however come a little easier. Come to think of it, self-love and self-care are voice lessons too. A while ago we made plans to join dear friends for dinner. It sounded good at the time. An hour before it was time to leave for their house, it didn't. An evening at home in front of the fire was just what my inner-doctor ordered. Just about then the phone rang. It was Kristine. "I'm calling to un-invite you. We are exhausted." "Perfect," I answered. "You saved me from having to cancel." I was ready to make that call, but in the end, didn't have to. We were two friends trying to help each other be good to ourselves so we could be good to those we love, including each other. We've decided that one mark of true friendship is being able to un-invite one another.

At the beginning learning to care for ourselves feels like a radical act, kind of like staging our own revolution. No meaningful change throughout history has happened without a lot of rabble-rousers tiring of the status quo. To change the course of our own histories is no different. We have to become rebels for our own cause, knowing that it will ruffle a lot of feathers, including our own. Meeting our own needs often collides with those of others. It's uncomfortable for everyone as we begin to care for ourselves in new ways. Healthy self-care means discovering what we need in order to live more fully. It is about equipping ourselves well so that we are well equipped for the life we have, including loving and caring for others. It does not mean being self-centered. It means living from a centered self.

What does it mean to love and care for yourself? It's a universal question requiring a personal answer. What does it take for each of us to show up fully for our own lives? In writing this chapter I decided to carve out some time to consider just this question for myself, in this specific chapter of my life. Feel free to join me in this little exercise. In fact, stop reading, go get paper and pencil, and we'll do it together. If you're like me, even taking the time to think about the question feels like a selfish hurdle. But let's soldier on, shall we? Let's clear that hurdle together and list any and everything that comes to mind when you think about what you need to love and care for yourself well. Trust your gut, and just for grins, don't judge any of what appears on your list. That's another hurdle we can clear together, which totally calls for a group fist pump in the air!

In case you're wondering, here is my list:

- Time in my home, by myself.
- Time with my people.
- Exercise, real food, at least seven hours of sleep.
- A good book.
- Meaningful work.
- Meditation and prayer.
- A good cup of French press coffee to start the day. Every day.
- And, drinking less wine.

Now, it's your turn. What does it mean for you to

care well for yourself, so that you are able to show up fully for your own life?

Coming up with the list is the easy part. Living it, not so much. A competitor at heart with a slightly OCD need for order, I made a plan to win the self-care race. Why bother if I'm not gonna do it right? Right? (Don't pretend you don't know what I'm talking about either girlfriend!) On your mark. Get set. Go!

- ◦ One entire day a week at home with no one else around.
- ◦ Weekly date night with Tom and regular phone calls with those I love.
- ◦ Two hours at the gym 6 days a week, home cooked organic meals every night.
- ◦ In bed by 9 to read, and up before dawn to meditate, pray and linger over that first cup of coffee.
- ◦ Knee deep in work that matters.
- ◦ Wine only once a week.

Talk about doomed from the start. Too little time, energy, and support. Too many responsibilities, relationships, and commitments. The hurdles between us and our lists can seem impossible to jump. Better to start small. Small step(s) = Big shift(s). Small steps are how we build momentum in a new direction. Choose just one thing on that list and find a way to bring even a teaspoonful more of self-care to the day. Maybe one thing will lead to another, since one thing is the way anything begins. Recently, I read a story of a beautiful piece of art, comprised of Japanese letters that read, "Each step is the place to learn."[60] Maybe it's never too late to learn to try a little tenderness. The key must be in the deciding.

So, I am learning to give myself grace to do what I am able. Thirty minutes at the gym is better than none. Take-out and a kiss as we fall into bed at night instead of dinner and a movie keep our flame alive. Or, at least an ember. Waking up in a hotel room on a business trip is better with the French press coffee maker I pack in my suitcase. Any work that I do matters with the right intention. Five minutes of meditation can be the eye in any storm. Short prayers work as well as long ones. Probably better. Writer and personal hero, Anne Lamott[61], says there are only three essential prayers we will ever need:

- Help.
- Thanks.
- Wow.

Those can be managed on even the most grueling of days.

- Only two glasses of wine. Help!
- Sometimes only one. Thanks!.
- On many nights, none. Wow!

13

HOMEWARD BOUND

What do we really crave more than wine?

⌇

"There's no place like home."[62]

DOROTHY

I TURNED 60 THE YEAR I began writing this book. It was a good milestone for reflecting back, taking stock of now, and looking to the road ahead. The night of my birthday I was surrounded by those who matter most to me. Gathered together in our rustic home in the Cascade mountains of Washington state, flooded with gratitude and humbled by the love and care in the room, "blessed" was the only word that came to mind. Maybe it was entering a new decade. Maybe it was having two of our daughters married in the past couple of years and another with a wedding in the works. Perhaps it was knowing that I am modeling the way for the next generation. Maybe it was recognizing that while I am strong and healthy today and married to the greatest guy ever, there are no guarantees beyond the present moment. Whatever the reason, it was time to consider the topic of this book: Women and wine. Starting with me. Because even in the midst of all of that love and celebration, joy and gratitude, as glasses were raised high to toast my life, deep down I knew that wine had a hold, and I wanted to loosen its grip. It was, I decided, a birthday present I could give to myself. And did.

It was a two-year process of unwrapping my relationship with wine. Where did it start? Why did it continue? What thirst was I trying to quench with it? What sent me looking for a(nother) glass of it? What did I lose because of it?

Every answer pointed in the same direction.

Home.

Even as a little girl I was what you would call a homebody. That hasn't changed much. One time, Kristine and I attended a workshop where participants were asked to create a visual picture of their perfect day. There were piles of magazines and images, scissors, glue and poster boards. Music played in the background, and there was to be no talking. In our perfectly imagined days there were no boundaries or restrictions. Without the limits of time, distance, money, and responsibilities, like magicians we could wave our wands and create the days of our dreams.

A couple of hours later we were all seated in a circle, and one by one, each woman shared her day with the rest of us. The days that were shared spanned the globe as someone would start their day with pastries and an espresso in Paris, take a morning hike through the Amazon, lunch on a beach Down Under, have a luxurious massage and late afternoon nap at a health spa on the Mediterranean, and end the evening watching the sun go down over the African savannah. Each day was filled with time travel as they wandered to the far corners of the earth. The two of us shared our days last. Neither one of us ever left home. Kindred spirits, home was where we each wanted to be more than anything. As Maya Angelou said, "I long, as does every human being, to be at home wherever I find myself."[63] That, I think, just about sums up what I have discovered since my evening walk. I just want to be home.

Home in my own skin.

Home in my own heart and mind and soul.

Home in my own life.

The only way to find that home is to stop running away from it. Wine has been a way to flee to another place, an escape from whatever is going on that is uncomfortable, a path to what seems an easier road or greener pastures. But home isn't "out there," it is only and always "in here." Like the Simon and Garfunkel song, we all long to be Homeward Bound[64]. That is where our music is playing. That is where our love lays waiting.

My girls will tell you that I am fond of saying, "We all have our shit." What I mean by that wise and expert opinion, is that we all have work to do to understand who we are, what we care about, how we want to show up in the world, who we want to love and what we want to do with the time we have. In order to do that we have to be willing to show up completely, bringing the good, the bad and the ugly of who we are to the sober light of day, and decide what to do with what we have. Nothing is harder, and nothing more important than becoming our truest, most authentic selves.

Every one of us, starting with me, has broken places and imperfections, wounds and unsightly blemishes. We've made choices that have set us on a crash course to injury and suffering, to ourselves and those we love. There are also things in life that get handed to us, like it or not. It's never fair and it totally sucks. Recently, I heard Oprah say that another thing she knows for sure is that "everything that happens to you, is also happening for you."[65] It made me want to bitch slap her on the spot. Except, I love her, and, I believe she's right. I am able to let the truth of those words sink in, if, I understand them in this way: Shit happens. It does. But, it does NOT happen to us to teach us a lesson. God doesn't look down, or up or out from wherever She or He is and say, "I think I'm going to teach you a lesson missy, and throw some cancer your way. Or, maybe burn your house down, take your child from you, break the trust in your marriage or get you fired. Let's see what you do with them apples." No. Stuff just plain happens to us. The only way it can happen for us is through our response to it. To let the pain and heartaches, challenges and train wrecks work their way through us, rather than trying to escape them through wine or any other means.

By being in the midst of our own lives, all that comes our way can transform us, making us more whole, more authentic, more human. It isn't easy work, this becoming fully ourselves. It is however, the best and most essential work we will ever do. Rumi said, "Through love, all pain turns to medicine." The love of others, the love of God, and perhaps first and foremost, the love we extend to ourselves, are the beginning of that alchemy. Love of wine is a poor substitute.

The awareness that came to me that evening on our road was a wake-up call, an invitation to bring my decades old wine habit up into the light of a new day. Curiosity was the first rung of the ladder out of my cellar, and it continues to show me the next one. And the next and the next and the next. As I wrote about it, I began to talk about it. The more I wrote and the more I talked, the less hold wine had. Talking about it with trusted others in my life has kept me honest. Writing about it as honestly as I've been able has kept me vulnerable. Being vulnerable has kept me connected to my questions and helped me find my way further up the ladder to the answers. It is our secrets that keep us locked up. When what has been kept in darkness comes to the light it can be transformed. Such transformation requires a willingness to step into our own darkness, to wedge our inner doors open, creating a crack through which, as Leonard Cohen sings, the "light gets in."[66] Today, my relationship with wine is no longer a secret affair. It is an open, honest, and dare-I-say, healthy relationship that no longer needs to be kept hidden. In the years still left I plan to live with the end in mind. When all is said and done, I want to have been present for my life. All of it. The pain and the joy, the heartache and the healing, the failures and the accomplishments, the miles and the moments, the miraculous and the mundane. Going forward, to the best of my ability, I intend to collect memories and not regrets.

My mom was a collector. Antique Roseville vases, delicate English china cups, primitive Redware mixing bowls. Almost every one of them a collector's item and, almost every one of them cracked and chipped. I used to think that she bought the cracked ones because they were the only ones she could afford. Maybe so. But I've also come to think that she saw beauty in the broken, the chipped, the imperfect, and the process of carefully gluing each piece back together was her act of love.

Maybe we are like precious cracked vessels, and the glue that puts our pieces back together, the liquid gold that mends our souls, comes from the courage and the grace to experience, not escape from our pain. Wine as a painkiller doesn't allow us to put the broken pieces of our life back together. Checking out with wine is a getaway car from the only home we can ever truly know. Too much wine and we can't get it together to show up and do what it takes to be our self and sing our song.

Wine has been my "thing." For others, it may stake no claim and I raise my glass to them. But. Something does. Whether addiction to our smart phone or binge watching the latest hit series, smoking pot every night or online shopping when no one else is awake, perfectionism or endless productivity, serving others but ignoring ourselves, nightly cocktails or an overflowing social calendar, excessive exercise or a fist full of peanut butter cups, a common thread in the fabric of the human soul is the temptation to avoid pain and discomfort. Whatever our means of escape, we flee at our own peril, the peril of those we love, and the peril of the entire world. Our job is to discover who we are and then hang on for dear life. When we don't, we pay dearly, and the price we pay is our song.

The world needs your song.

Your song wants to be sung.

You are the only one who can sing it.

Sing it, Sister!
Sing it!

AFTERWORD

෮

Whether you turn to the right or to the left,
your ears will hear a voice behind you, saying,
"This is the way; walk in it."

ISAIAH 30:21

AWARENESS IS THE BEGINNING of change. The transformation of my relationship with wine started before I ever sat down to write one word of this book. It began to change on that evening walk, at the bend in our road. From that moment on, it could never be the same. I might be able to fool others, but I could no longer fool myself. The wine I drank had become a coping mechanism, a daily habit quietly wrapped in lovely ritual.

Much of the writing took place as I continued to drink wine on a regular, although more mindful, basis. However, for the past eight months, I haven't had any wine. Not one glass. Which is not to say that I haven't wanted to pour a glass or three on many an evening. And yet, in finishing this book and in keeping with my commitment to be curious, it felt an important and necessary act of integrity. The final writing needed to take place without my nightly wine. What could I learn about my relationship with wine by not drinking any?

There were, of course, some basic, practical things that came with not drinking wine. Better sleep, a few pounds shed, increased clarity of thought, and more money in our bank account. Fine. Those are all well and good, and I'm grateful. But of course, none of those nice benefits are the reason I decided to take this all on.

- ❧ I took it on because I had to.

- ❧ I took it on because I could no longer ignore what I had known, somewhere in the deep recesses of my heart, to be true all along.

- ❧ I took it on because the message on my evening walk was the next closest thing to getting hit over the head with a wine bottle, and had I ignored it, I'm pretty sure that would have been the next step. The truth finally made its way through my defenses and rationalizations, my excuses and justifications, and I simply had no choice but to RSVP to the invitation with the only possible answer. "Yes. Yes, I will come to the party."

Without wine, here is what I have learned:

⊸ **I have learned** that the choice to explore my relationship with wine was the hardest choice. When it comes to making any kind of meaningful change, you're not ready until you're ready. Until that moment on the road, I hadn't been ready, because I knew that once that choice was made, I could no longer drink wine without wondering if, on this particular evening, at the end of this particular day, and in these particular circumstances, is this glass of wine a good thing or a bad thing?

⊸ **I have learned** that there are plenty of nights that I don't give wine a second thought nor do I even miss it. That discovery came as a big surprise. More like a total shock to be honest with you. What would I do when it came time to take that lovely glass off the shelf, uncork the bottle, pour an ample glass, take that first sip, and feel welcomed home? I'd done it for so long, I couldn't imagine the evening feeling anything but empty, unfamiliar, boring, and uncomfortable without it. As it turned out however, there are plenty of other ways to mark the end of a day: An evening walk, a game of backgammon with Tom, a leisurely phone call with someone I love, the next episode of that favorite series, a good book, some time at the piano, putting in a few more hours of writing, or simply a simple evening as night quietly descends.

↶ **I have learned** that there are also plenty of nights when wine is my first, second and third thought, and I miss that lovely glass of wine with a thirst that feels like nothing else will do. It has become crystal clear that any mental or emotional pain, discomfort or unease can threaten my resolve to leave the wine in the bottle. There are nights that I yell, to no one in particular, "I'd KILL for a glass of wine! RIGHT NOW!" And then I take a deep breath. That seductive craving for wine has become a signal of an inner thirst.

↶**I have learned** that I can sit with my own discomfort through the practice of noticing and naming. As I notice and name whatever I am feeling – loneliness, restlessness, irritation, resentment, boredom, sadness, fear, whatever the uncomfortable feelings du jour – I have the capacity to sit with and learn from them, rather than drink up and check out.

↶**I have learned** that feeling inner pain is how I discover what is in need of care. Pain is a lens, focusing a light on that which needs my attention. It opens a doorway to inner healing and well-being. The pain we ignore can lead to greater injury, and it always, always, always seeps out into the world, and into the lives of those around us, starting with those we love the most.

↶**I have learned** that I still love wine.

↜I **have learned** that I can enjoy it differently.

And...

↜I **have learned** that when Truth comes knocking, the good choice, the courageous choice, the life-giving choice, is to unlock the door, open it wide, and throw away the key.

ACKNOWLEDGEMENTS

~

"It is in the shelter of each other that the people live."

IRISH PROVERB

LIKE EVERYTHING ELSE that I've ever accomplished in my life, I could never have written this book without the help, support, and shelter of others. The generosity, honesty and amazing grace I have received along the way has been overwhelming and humbling.

It took me awhile to gather the courage to even begin talking about writing this book, knowing that once I actually gave voice to the idea, I could never go back. The first person I finally found the courage to talk with about it was my dear friend, David Berry, who has taught me so much about the power of the voice. Thank you David for being the kind of person who could hold a safe space for me to speak up, and for stopping me mid-sentence and telling me to "write it now and write it raw". Know that I heeded your words, and called upon them when I grew faint of heart.

Once in motion, the support I needed showed up exactly on time. I am indebted to The Glenwood Girls (you know who you are) for your love, laughter and loyalty. Thank you for gathering around the fire, fanning my creative embers, and keeping life real. There were those who carefully read what I wrote, and through their honest and thoughtful feedback, made me a better writer and this a better book. Some of you endured my "shitty first drafts"[67], others read later versions, and some of you brave souls did both. My profound thanks to Caley Moyer for reading every word and taking the time to pour her heart, soul and wonderful brain into rich feedback. For any and all of the reading that you did, thank you too to Kristine Van Raden, David Berry, Barb Bell, Bridget McLaughlin, Pam Shelley, Tia Ribary, Kelly Ryan, Alia Fitzgerald, and Barb Young. And of course, thank you Tom Pierson for loving me by reading, editing, and listening patiently to my thoughts. It would not have happened without you. Thank you to my editor, Lori Anne Rising. Your love of this book, and your attention to detail mean the world. To my partner in publishing, Nancy Cleary of Wyatt-MacKenzie, thank you for loving this book from day one, and for helping me make it happen. The crossing of our paths was no accident. Thank you to Ali Towle Moore for encouraging me to go pitch my idea at the Willamette Writer's Conference. It scared the hell out of me, so of course I knew that I had to do it. Massive thanks to Barb Bell (aka Nash), my fearless and brilliant friend. You always extend ease, space and grace to me, and, you will always be on my 1x1 square of paper. Thank you to Katie Meleney of Practical Beauty for helping me create a beautiful and sacred space to write. Thank you to Dave and Lizzy for reminding me to always be courageous enough to tell the truth. To David Van Raden, my brilliant friend, thank you for thinking of the perfect title, reminding us that when all else fails "to just go outside" and for being a quiet constant I can always count on.

It may be unorthodox to thank some whom I've never met, but their support along my way was profound. In the early morning hours over my pre-dawn cup of French press coffee, I was fed and fortified by the writings of Barbara Brown Taylor, Anne Lamott, Krista Tippet, Rachel Naomi Remen, Elizabeth Gilbert, Seth Godin, Parker Palmer, Pema Chödrön, Sue Bender, and Richard Rohr.

Finally, there are two women, without whom I might not make it through another day. To my one and only sister Margie – you prayed me into the world, and you've never stopped. Thank you for generously and fiercely loving me and mine every single day. And, to my one and only dearest and best friend, Kristine Van Raden – thank you for saying "yes" to dinner all those years ago, for walking by my side and living in my heart ever since, for loving me no matter what, and for always letting me drink the "good" wine.

ABOUT THE AUTHOR

↬

"Where there is great love there
are always miracles…"[68]
WILLA CATHER

MOLLY DAVIS is a writer, speaker, facilitator and coach, with over twenty years of national and international experience. She is the founder of Trailhead Coaching & Consulting, and through her work, helps people to courageously step more fully into their own lives by connecting who they are with what they do. For 18 years she has worked as a senior facilitator for Learning Point Group (http://learningpointinc.com), teaching primarily on leadership and supervisory development.

Molly is co-author of the internationally published *Letters to Our Daughters*, written with her best friend, Kristine Van Raden. Highlighted on the Oprah Show, the book is a collection of letters from women to their daughters, and shines a light on the common threads that connect us as human beings regardless of circumstances. As a result of their cross-country book tour and subsequent invitations to speak, they founded Matters That Matter® (http://mattersthatmatter.com), a partnership to provide keynotes, retreats and workshops designed to inspire others to live according to what they care about. Their work has taken them to national conventions, annual fundraisers, and world-class health spas, including Rancho La Puerta near San Diego, California.

Molly lives with her husband Tom at the base of Mt. Adams in Washington State. She loves nothing more than gathering family and friends together in their rustic home to eat good food, engage in real and sometimes raucous conversation, savor some good wine, and find rest, connection, and renewal together. Most days you will find her in jeans and well-worn cowboy boots.

You can find Molly at:
trailheadcoachingandconsulting.com
twitter.com/@MollyLDavis
facebook.com/MollyDavisAuthor

A READER'S GUIDE

∽

Questions for personal reflection and group discussion.

"The soul speaks its truth only under quiet, inviting,
and trustworthy conditions." [69]

PARKER PALMER

INTRODUCTION

It all started on that evening walk at a bend in the
road. As much as a wake-up call to an unhealthy relationship with wine, it was in invitation to begin a new
trail of discovery deeper into my own life. I believe that
we are all here to live lives of purpose and meaning,
and, to live as authentically and wholeheartedly as we
can possibly muster. It is what we are called to do. It is
who we are called to be. Anything that gets in the way
of that calling deserves our full attention. Wine was getting in my way. Today it isn't.

It is my heartfelt hope that this book has served you

well. Perhaps you are at a bend in your own road and would like to explore further. If so, these questions are designed to help you, and perhaps some trusted others in your life, along your own trail of discovery.

CHAPTER 1

Is sharing some wine together a part of your connection with friends?

"It is an exploration of when and why I choose to drink wine to dull pain, avoid discomfort, cope with stress, and check out of reality. And why other women might do the same." (pg. 2) What is your reaction to this statement? Do you see yourself in these words? If so, how?

Molly says that there are two basic reasons she pours a glass of wine: To celebrate, and to checkout. How would you describe your own reasons for drinking wine?

Do you ever wonder if you sometimes drink too much wine? Do you talk about it with anyone else? Why or why not?

On pages 8–12, Molly lists numerous women she has encountered over the years that seem to share her love of wine. Do see yourself anywhere in that list? Are there some examples from your own experience that suggest women like their wine... maybe a little too much?

CHAPTER 2

Can you trace the thread of your own wine drinking habit?

When you pour a glass of wine, what does it signify for you?

Molly says, *"If my wine had a name, the label on the bottle would say 'Home'. (pg. 19)* What would your wine label say?

What sends you looking for a glass of wine?

CHAPTER 3

When you think about "your song", what does that mean to you?

"When in danger of getting lost in a life that isn't ours... our song takes us back home where we belong." (pg. 22) What do you think of this notion? Can you think of times when your own 'song' has brought you back to yourself?

Are there places/times/relationships in your life where you choose to silence your own song? Why and at what cost to yourself? Do you ever use wine as a way to lessen the impact of losing your own song?

"When the song is ours, the ground upon which we stand is always holy, because our song isn't a performance. It is an offering."(pg. 27) What do these words mean to you?

What is the gift of song that you can offer to the world? What and who will be impacted if your music remains silent?

CHAPTER 4

How would you answer the following two questions about your own experiences of sorrow and loss? "When did I use wine as a deadbolt, losing the chance to discover what they had to reveal, both in and for me? When did I unlock my interior door and welcome them in as unexpected guests bearing gifts?" (pg. 30)

"To be human is to, at times, find ourselves filled with sorrow and sadness along our way." Do you agree with this statement? What are some times of sorrow and sadness that you have experienced? How did you manage those times? What role did wine play or not play in navigating your sorrow?

She tells the story of losing her horses. Can you think of a time that you lost some part of yourself? How did it happen? How did you cope with that loss?

When sorrow hits, do you see it as an *"invitation to or a retreat from"?* (pg. 36)

CHAPTER 5

"We have multiple hats to wear, balls to juggle and pieces to hold together." (pg. 39) What are the roles and expectations that fill your life? How would you describe the hats you wear/balls you juggle/pieces you hold together?

"We hide our wine in plain sight, drinking from lovely glasses for all to see. It helps us look the part, even if inside we are falling apart because we can't meet all of those expectations, and have lost sight of our own lives." (pg. 39) Does this ring true in your own experience.

When you think about meeting expectations, do you feel like you are working to live up to the expectations of others over your own?

On page 41, Molly describes how we often accumulate unexamined expectations, similar to how our garages get overcrowded with accumulated material things. Do you relate to that idea? How might you go about accessing the expectations you've gathered along the way, and deciding which ones to keep and which ones to discard?

Similar to her experience described on pages 43–45, can you think of a time when meeting the expectations of someone else caused you to lose your way for a long time?

CHAPTER 6

Do you or other women you know struggle with having a positive body image?

What is your reaction to the writing on the dressing room mirror that said, *"Use kind words."* (pg. 47) When was the last time you used kind words to yourself when you looked in the mirror? What kind words might you begin saying to yourself?

On page 48 Molly talks about a magazine article in which "Before" and "After" photos of Jamie Lee Curtis were displayed. What are your thoughts about that? Does the cultural standard set in the media negatively impact your self-image?

"When did it become not okay to age? When did it become okay not to age?" (pg. 48). How do you feel about aging? Do you feel pressure to look younger than your age?

Molly talks about working with a trainer as a 60 year old women to *"...find the body that is mine."* Do you relate to that desire? What would that mean to you at this stage in your life?

CHAPTER 7

Is your experience of being a mom different than you anticipated? In what ways, good, bad or otherwise?

Do you feel pressure to be the "right kind of mom"? Where do those pressures and expectations come from?

On page 57, motherhood is described as a two-sided coin. On one side all the good things, on the flip side, all of the challenging and difficult things. How does that coin land in your experience?

Do you drink wine as a way to get through another evening? What about other moms you know? Do you talk about it with each other?

"You are only as happy as your unhappiest child." (pg. 65) In your experience, is there truth to that statement?

CHAPTER 8

If you work outside of the home, what other responsibilities do you juggle? If you don't work outside the home, do you feel the pressure to do so? Are you part of what is referred to as the "sandwich generation", caring for both your children and one or more parents?

Do work and family pressures often send you looking for a glass (or more) of wine?

What do you think of the notion that, *"Our lives are best served when we are able to connect who we are with what we do and how we do it."*? *(pg. 73)* How does that idea correspond to how you live your life today?

Can you relate to the following: *"Raise your hand if you've ever left work, looking forward to nothing more than that first sip of wine; to the relaxation that happens as the knots in your stomach begin to loosen their grip, the anxiety that begins to ease, the frustration that drops down a notch, the resentment that gets sent to bed early without supper, the fear of failure that momentarily fades away, and the stress that with each mouthful becomes a little less stressful. All when you pour that first glass of wine. Keep your hand up if you've also ever walked into the house after work, gone straight to the kitchen, and poured yourself a glass of wine before ever taking your off your coat or unloading the groceries (which, of course, includes another bottle of wine just in case it's been "one of those days")".* *(pg. 74)* Is your hand still in the air? Do you know other women who might relate to this?

What do you think of the idea that we need to *"...find*

our way to work that matters or work in a way that matters regardless of where we find ourselves?" How does this statement align with your own situation?

CHAPTER 9

Chapter 9 opens with these two sentences: *"Love is kind of like a home for your heart. Like any house, it is best built with a good design, on a strong foundation, using quality materials."* What do you think of that idea? When it comes to love, what constitutes a strong foundation, good design and quality materials?

Molly describes her own criteria early in her life when looking for love (*pg. 83*). Do you relate to that in your own experience? What would you tell your younger self about how to find the kind of love you are looking for?

Have you ever used wine as a way to avoid thinking about how, when it comes to love, you might have settled for less than you deserve? Has wine helped you forget or pretend that you feel "stuck" in a relationship?

What do you think about the point made that, when it comes to love, we settle for less because we are afraid? Can you relate to any of the list of reasons she gives on page 86–87?

How do we first learn to *"...walk in partnership with our own soul..."* so that we are then able to better choose an equal partner?

CHAPTER 10

What do you think about the idea that *"We are each tiny little creators, speaking our own lives into being."*? (pg. 91) How can you see that playing out in your own life?

Are there times and situations in your own life where speaking up with your authentic voice is difficult, where, as Molly wonders, you *"...didn't speak up, take a stand or make a different choice?* What does it feel like or cost you when you keep your true voice silent?

On pages 97–98, she talks about using a 3x5 card as a tool to help her speak up in a situation where she found it hard to do so. Are there areas in your own life where a 3x5 card could help you speak up and use your voice in a new and more powerful way?

Do you agree that our inner voice is always available to us, that we can find and hear it if we choose to get quiet and listen? Can you think of any places in your own life where your voice is speaking to you?

Does another glass of wine ever help you avoid important conversations, choices or changes?

CHAPTER 11

Has too much wine ever caused you to miss creating a meaningful memory? Has it caused you to do or say something that you later regret?

Have you been able to extend grace to yourself for those times?

What do you think about the view that those experiences, when too much wine led to either forgotten memories or remembered regrets, are able to teach us valuable lessons for the future? Can you think of a time when that has been true for you?

When it comes to how you use wine, what would it mean for you to, "Begin with the end in mind"? (pg. 105)

Does your relationship with wine sometimes get in the way of your ability to be present for yourself and others?

CHAPTER 12

Is it difficult for you to care well for yourself? Do you find it hard to tend to your own needs over those of others? What feelings do you experience as a result?

Does wine at the end of a day feel like an act of self-care? Are there times when it actually is? Do you ever use it as a way to compensate for giving too much of yourself away?

Like Molly (*pgs. 111–113*), can you remember a time when caring for your own needs first was really hard, and yet you did it anyway? What emotions did you experience, and what was it that allowed you to take care of yourself over someone else's needs?

How do you respond to the following: "*It is about equipping ourselves well so that we are well equipped for the life we have, including loving and caring for others. It does not mean being self-centered. It means living from a centered self*"?

What does good self care mean, specifically, for you? Is there one thing you would like to begin doing as an act of self-care? How could you begin?

CHAPTER 13

How would you describe the role wine plays in your life today?

"*Where did it start? Why did it continue? What thirst was I trying to quench with it? What sent me looking for a(nother) glass of it? What did I lose because of it?*

Molly says that for her, the answer to each of those questions is summed up in the same word: Home. Is there one word that would answer all of those questions for you?

What do you think about the possibility that, *"everything that happens to us also happens for us"*? How do you see that at work in your own experience?

What have you learned about your own relationship with wine as you have read this book? What were your reasons for choosing to read it in the first place?

Do you agree with Molly when she says, *"…a common thread in the fabric of the human soul is the temptation to avoid pain and discomfort"*? In what ways do you see this happening in the lives of others? Does wine help you avoid pain and discomfort?

Are there changes you would like to make in when and why you drink wine? How would you describe the kind of relationship you would like to have with wine?

ENDNOTES

[1] John O'Donohue. *Beauty: The Invisible Embrace* (New York: Harper Collins, 2005), 23.

[2] Host:Robin Young. "New Thinking On Women and Alcohol." Here And Now. January 20, 2014.

[3] *Friday Night Lights*. Developed by Peter Berg. Executive Produced by Brian Grazer, David Nevins, Sarah Aubry, Jason Katims. Based on the non-fiction book by H.G. Bissinger. Produced by NBCUniversal. Premiered: 2006

[4] Annie Dillard. *The Writing Life*. (New York: Harper Collins 2013), 32.

[5] Nadia Bolz-Weber, *Accidental Saints: Finding God in All the Wrong People* (New York:Convergent Books, an imprint of Crown Publishing Group, a division of Penguin Random House LLC. 2015), 172.

[6] Gilbert, Elizabeth. *Big Magic: Creative Living Beyond Fear (New York*: Riverhead Books. 2015), 221.

[7] *Songs in The Key of Life*. Produced by Stevie Wonder. Motown Records: 1976

[8] Krista Tippet. Maria Popova – Cartographer of Meaning in a Digital Age: *On Being*. (Distributed by PRX) May 14, 2015

[9] *Holy Ground*. Written by Geron Davis, 1994

[10] Rachel Naomi Remen. *Kitchen Table Wisdom* (New York, Riverhead Books, 10th Anniversary Edition, 2006) 76-77.

[11] Ann Staley, *Instructions For The Wishing Light* (Seattle, Washington: Booktrope, 2013), 109.

[12] https://theheartofawakening.wordpress.com/2013/07/10/poem-of-the-week-the-guest-house-by-rumi/

[13] http://www.merriam-webster.com/dictionary/sorrow

[14] Barbara Brown Taylor. *Learning to Walk in the Dark,* (New York. Harper Collins, 2014), 80.

[15] *Groundhog Day.* Directed by Harold Ramis. Producerd by Trevor Albert, Harold Ramis. Screenplay by Danny Rubin, Harold Ramis. Story by Danny Rubin. United States: Columbia Pictures, 1993

[16] http://www.pemberley.com/janeinfo/ppv3n60.html

[17] *The Sound of Music.* Directed by Robert Wise, Screen Play written by Ernest Lehman, George Hurdalek,. United States: 20th Century Fox, 1965.

[18] Eve Ensler. AZQuotes.com, Wind and Fly LTD, 2016. http://www.azquotes.com/quote/876477,

[19] Wallace, Amy. "Jamie Lee Curtis: True Thighs. *MORE Magazine, September 2002*

[20] Anne Lamott. *Bird by Bird: Some Instructions on Writing and Life* (New York: Pantheon Books, 1994), 137.

[21] http://www.goodreads.com/quotes/197442-if-you-love-somebody-let-them-go-for-if-they

[22] *One Flew Over The Cuckoo's Nest.* Directed by Milos' Forman. Screenplay written by Lawrence Hauben, Bo Goldman. Produced by Saul Zaentz, Michael Douglas. United States: Warner Bros., 1975

[23] Kipling,Rudyard. BrainyQuote.com, Xplore Inc, 2016. http://www.brainyquote.com/quotes/quotes/r/rudyardkip118509.html.

[24] Brown, Brene: The Power of Vulnerabilility. TEDxHouston June 2010.https://www.ted.com/talks/brene_brown _on_vulnerability/transcript?language=en#t-1067334

[25] Thatcher, Margaret. BrainyQuote.com.http://www.brainyquote.com/quotes/quotes/m/margaretth127088.html..

[26] US Department of Labor. *Women's Bureau. http://www.dol.gov/wb/stats/25mostcommon_occs_employ_women.txt.htm.*

[27] http://www.dol.gov/wb/stats/ususal_weekly_hrs_sex+2014_txt.htm.

[28] http://www.dol.gov/wb/stats//laborforce_participation_rate_mothers_age_marital_2014_txt.htm.

[29] Rampell,Catherine.*U.S. Women on the Rise as Family Breadwinner* http://www.nytimes.com/2013/05/30/business/economy/women-as-family-breadwinner-on-the-rise-study-says.html?_r=0

[30] http://www.ted.com/talks/sheryl_sandberg_why_we_have_too_few_women_leaders/transcript?language=en. 11:22

[31] TED. https://www.ted.com/talks/jessica_shortall_how_america_fails_new_parents_and_their_babies?language=en

[32] Family Caregiver Alliance. https://www.caregiver.org/women-and-caregiving-facts-and-figures

[33] Cameron, Julia, *The Artist's Way: A Spiritual Path to Higher Creativity,* (New York: G.P. Punam's Sons, 1992).

[34] Gide, Andre. BrainyQuotes.com. http://www.brainyquote.com/quotes/authors/a/andre_gide.html.

[35] Van Raden, Kristine, Davis, Molly. *Letters to Our Daughters: Mother's Words of Love* (Hillsboro, OR Beyond Words Publishing. 1997. New York, NY. Hyperion. 1999)

[36] www.mattersthatmatter.com

[37] Krauss, Nicole. *The History of Love*. (New York, NY. W.W. Norton & Company, 2005), 242.

[38] *Fiddler on The Roof*. Directed by Norman Jewison. Produced by Norman Jewison,, Walter Mirisch (uncredited). Screenplay by Joseph Stein. Based on the book: *Tevye and His Daughters* by Sholem Aleichem. United States: United Artists 1971

[39] https://en.wikipedia.org/wiki/Tinder_(app)

[40] Match.com. http://www.match.com/cpx/en-us/match/IndexPage/

[41] FarmersOnly.com. http://farmersonly.com

[42] Amish-Online Dating.com. http://amish-online-dating.com

[43] GlutenFreeSingles. http://www.glutenfreesingles.com

[44] http://www.huffingtonpost.com/jennifer-gauvain/doubts-before-marriage_b_919868.html

[45] *The Bridal Chorus (Here Comes The Bride or The Bridal March..* Composer? Richard Wagner. From the 1850 opera *Lohengrin*.

[46] Sally Field winning an Oscar® for "Places in the Heart", YouTube. 57th Annual Awards® in 1985. https://www.youtube.com/watch?v=nQSIIk-_das

[47] Schnarsch, David. *Passionate Marriage: Sex, Love , and Intimacy In Emotionally Committed Relationships*. New York: W.W. Norton & Company, 1997

[48] Weintraub, Pam. "How to Grow Up: The roadmap for how to become an authentic adult is also a blueprint for putting passion back in relationships." *Psychology Today*. May 1,2012. https://www.psychologytoday.com/articles/201205/how-grow

[49] Albright, Madeleine. BrainyQuote.com. http://www.brainyquote.com/quotes/quotes/m/madeleinea432621.html.

[50] Gn.1:3 New Oxford Annotated Bible

[51] Berry, David. Preface to *A More Daring Life: Finding Voice at the Crossroads of Change*, (San Bernardino, CA. Publisher: Author. 2016), vi-vii.

[52] *The King's Speech*. Directed by Tom Hooper, Screen Play written by David Seidler. United States, September 2010

[53] *A River Runs Through It*. Directed by Robert Redford. Produced by Jake Eberts, Robert Redford, Patrick Markey. Screenplay by Richard Friedenberg. Based on the novella *A River Runs Throuhg It* by Norman Maclean. United States: Columbia Pictures 1992

[54] The Book of Common Prayer. *Evening Prayer I* (New York: Oxford University,.Date unkown), 63.

[55] Obama, Michelle. National Womens Council. http://nationalwomenscouncil.org/health.php

[56] *I Am Woman*. Helen Reddy. Written by Ray Burton, Helen Reddy. Produced by Jay Senter. Capitol Records 1972

[57] New Oxford Annotated Bible NRSV, Matthew 22: 39

[58] https://www.goodreads.com/author/quotes/86608.Lucille_Ball

[59] *Defending The Caveman*. Written by Rob Becker. Premiered: San Francisco, 1991

[60] Bender, Sue. *Everyday Sacred: A Woman's Journey Home*. (USA:HarperSanFrancisco - An Imprint of HarperCollins, 1995), 18.

[61] Lamott, Anne. *Help Thanks Wow: The Three Essential Prayers*. (New York: Riverhead Books, 2012)

[62] https://en.wikiquote.org/wiki/The_Wizard_of_Oz_(1939_film)

[63] Angelou, Maya. Goodreads. http://www.goodreads.com/quotes/277051-i-long-as-does-every-human-being-to-be-at

[64] *Homeward Bound*. Paul Simon, Art Garfunkel, From the album *Parsley, Sage, Rosemary and Thyme*. Columbia Records, 1996

[65] *Getting Unstuck: Creating a Limitless Life*. Oprah Winfrey, Deepok Chopra. Day 5: *Rising Above Your Old Conditioning* 00:48

[66] *Anthem*. Leonard Cohen. Album: The Future. Columbia Records, 1992

[67] Lamott, Anne. *Bird by Bird* (New York: Pantheon Books, 1994), 21.

[68] http://www.goodreads.com/work/quotes/1457974-death-comes-for-the-archbishop

[69] https://www.brainpickings.org/2014/12/02/parker-palmer-let-your-life-speak/